E I E I O

Written by Anne Cotton & Fran Martin

Illustrated by Lyn Hope

Teaching a Theme Using Whole Language Strategies

Published by
Teaching Resource Center
P.O. Box 1509
San Leandro, CA 94577

Printed in the United States of America
ISBN: 1–56785–016–2

Contents

The Basic Teaching Strategies

In the development of this theme you will find such phrases as **brainstorm for, develop in the pocket chart, sort and classify**, etc. To help clarify these phrases we have listed these basic teaching strategies and have given a brief description of each.

Fill with language:

This is when we read to the children. We read not only stories but poetry and factual information as well. We begin with a discussion of the illustrations to develop as much oral language as possible. We stop periodically to provide the opportunity for the child to anticipate and predict what might happen next. We also read a selection many times over to help make that selection become a part of the child. We feel strongly that we must continually *fill the child with language* as we move ahead with the theme.

Chanting:

Children need to work orally with the patterns of language. The primary way to do this with very young children is by chanting. This technique helps instill the rhythm and structure of language which then becomes a part of their everyday speech.

One way to chant is by using the my turn, your turn technique. The teacher reads a phrase and the children echo this phrase. The teacher tracks (runs hand under the text, pointing to each word) as the chanting takes place. Children may chant using the whole text (pictures, pictures and words, or words alone), or merely chant a repetitive phrase ("Not I," said the dog.) Chanting may be done using big books, charts, brainstorming ideas, pocket chart activities, trade books, etc. Songs and poems should also be included. When working with songs and poetry, we often add rhythmic hand movements which help instill the rhythm of the language and enhances the memorization.

Brainstorming:

Brainstorming is when children orally respond to a question posed by the teacher with the results usually being recorded where they may be seen by the children. This gives the teacher an insight into the children's knowledge. We usually begin a theme by brainstorming for what the children know about a given subject. A lack of ideas indicates that the children may need a *refill* of language and knowledge. The brainstorming is continuously being added to as the theme is developed.

Brainstorming is a whole class activity. The teacher begins by asking a question such as "What is green?" and elicits responses from the children. As the children respond, the teacher draws the appropriate pictures on the chalkboard and the children chant. **Note:** at the beginning of the kindergarten year, draw a picture only. No words are needed.

After the brainstorming, again chant all the pictures that were drawn: "A leaf is green. A turtle is green. Grass is green. A car is green." As the year progresses you will want to add words to the brainstorming:

Most brainstorming needs to be saved! As you work through a theme you will be continually referring to these ideas. Copy the brainstorming onto cards or chart paper. The cards may be displayed using masking tape, sticky side out. The chart may be used for matching and rebuilding. At a later date the chart may be cut apart and made into a strip book.

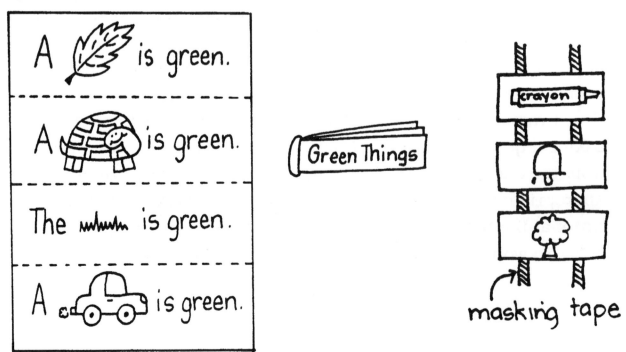

Another example of a brainstorming technique is to record ideas in categories that are not labeled. After the pattern is obvious, the children tell where to record the next idea. This method helps stimulate the children's thinking.

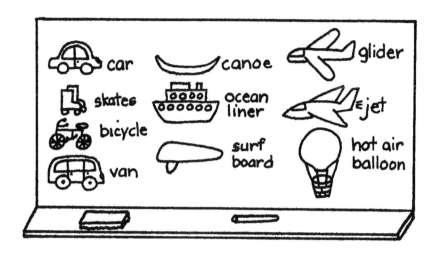

Sorting and Classifying:

This when children look for likenesses and differences and put things together that are alike in some manner. The ideas from brainstorming activities are ideal for sorting and classifying. We usually begin classifying with groups of four to six children, with each group having about twenty cards or items to sort.

After this small group sorting activity, the whole class regroups and chants. Example: we classified according to color and then chanted, "A chair is green. An olive is green. A fat frog is green, etc." Gradually, we work toward activities that will involve individual classifications. The results of these activities may be graphed, producing either a real graph or a pictorial graph.[1]

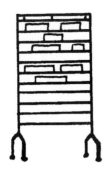

Develop in the Pocket Chart:

We use a pocket chart made of clear acetate and nylon.[2] You may use sentence strips or tagboard cards (laminated or contacted for a longer life) with the pocket chart. Whole texts, repeated phrases or pictures only may be used. There are a variety of ways to use the pocket chart. We listed our favorites:

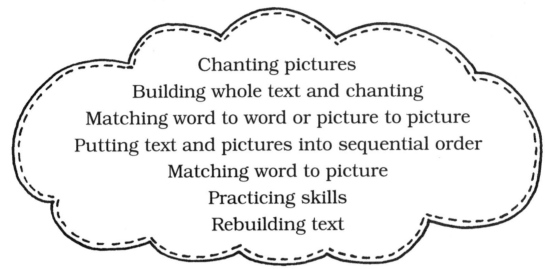

Chanting pictures
Building whole text and chanting
Matching word to word or picture to picture
Putting text and pictures into sequential order
Matching word to picture
Practicing skills
Rebuilding text

When we are developing a lesson in the pocket chart, we usually insert the appropriate pictures, or text and pictures, and then have the children chant **many** times. We may ask the children to hide their eyes and then we take something out of the text or merely turn it over.

The children then decide what is missing and chant to see if they are correct. We then take more than one word, picture, or phrase out (or turn them over) and repeat the process. The final task is to rebuild the entire text.

Samples:

Step 1:   Chanting pictures
             "A leaf is green."

v

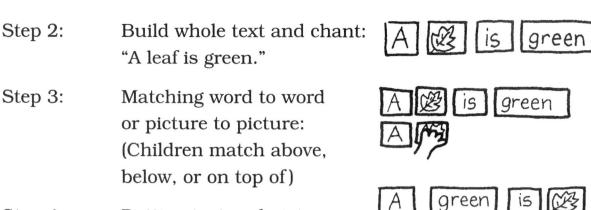

Step 2:   Build whole text and chant:
            "A leaf is green."

Step 3:   Matching word to word
            or picture to picture:
            (Children match above,
            below, or on top of)

Step 4:   Putting text and pictures
            into sequential order:

Step 5:   Matching word to picture:

Step 6:   Practicing skills:

- Find the word that says *green*.
- Find the word that says *is*.
- Find the word that comes before *green*.
- Find the word that comes after *is*.
- What sound do you hear at the
  beginning of the word *leaf*?

Step 7:   Rebuilding: all pictures and text are distributed to the
            children and the complete story is built again in the
            pocket chart. Children read the text from the pocket
            chart, checking for accuracy.

Tracking:

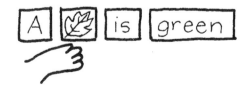

This involves moving your hand under
and pointing to each word as it is read.
This helps develop left to right pro-
gression as well as one-to-one correspondence between the printed text
and the spoken word.

Big Books:

These are enlarged versions of books, poems or songs. The print must be large enough so that it may be seen by the entire class. The enlarged print allows us to track as we read and helps to develop one-to-one correspondence. Many of the activities used with the pocket chart may also be used with big books. We laminate the pages of teacher-prepared big books and bind them with loose leaf rings. The rings may be taken out and the pages shuffled so that the children may sequence the big book. For obvious reasons **do not** number the pages. These books are really loved and used over and over by the children.

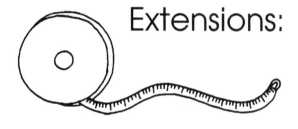

Extensions:

These are activities we practice what we learned during brainstorming, reading, chanting, and the various pocket chart activities. We try to incorporate the following:

Individual booklets – Each child makes his/her own booklet and should have the opportunity to read and track before taking it home.

Class book – Each child contributes a page and the book is kept in the classroom library.

Drama – Children act out the activity with **all** children taking **all** the parts. (a bit noisy but very effective)

Art – Children make illustrations for bulletin boards, booklets, plays, etc., using as many different kinds of art media as possible.

Make-a-play – Children retell a story by manipulating characters they have made.

Writing – All writing activities need to be extensively developed orally **first**.

1. Using a structure or frame, the children fill in the blanks by taking the ideas from the brainstorming activities.

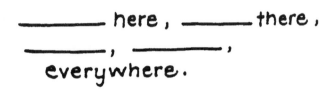

2. Creating innovations: children orally rewrite a familiar text using their own words. Example: (change "Brown bear, brown bear, what do you see?" to "Octopus, Octopus, what do you see?") This can be an individual or a whole group activity. The teacher may need to take dictation for the very young child.

3. Dictation: children individually illustrate and the teacher transcribes for them.

Draw with me – This is a whole class activity where language development is the goal. We do not consider this an art lesson. All the children are working with individual chalkboards at this time. We ask the children to name all the parts that need to be included to draw a specific object. A sample follows on the next page.

"What do we need to make a house?"

"A door"

"A roof"

"Windows"

(continue until entire picture is completed)

Individual sequencing – This is when each child puts pictures or a text into a specific order. This is usually a *cut and paste* activity. It varies in difficulty. We begin with pictures only, then pictures with the text, and finally the text alone. We also put the text in sequence with numerals, words, and pictures.

Pictures only:

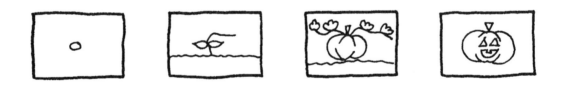

Pictures with text:

This is a seed.   This is a vine.   This is a pumpkin.   This is a jack o lantern.

text must be glued

Numeral, text and picture:

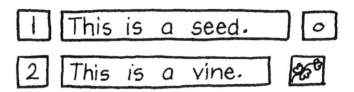

Homework – This is when we try to involve the family. The homework is occasional and we include a detailed explanation. This activity is returned to class and used for chanting, classifying booklet making or other language activities.

An example might be:

Dear Parents,

Our language arts theme this month is centered around plants. This week we are learning about seeds. Your child needs to bring a picture of something that grows from a seed. You may help your child draw or find a picture in a magazine. Please return the picture tomorrow.

Thank you for helping!

A follow-up activity might include sorting and classifying these pictures according to whether the plant produces food or not, i.e., flower, grapes, oak tree, oranges, etc. A booklet can then be made including all the homework pictures or individual booklets may be made from each classification.

— —

1. Baratta-Lorton, Mary. *Mathematics Their Way,* Addison-Wesley Publishing Company, Reading, MA 1976.
2. Available from **Teaching Resource Center**, P.O. Box 1509, 14023 Catalina St., San Leandro, CA 94577.

Theme At A Glance

Trade Books & Big Books

All About Animals
Baby Animals On The Farm
Bill Grogan's Boat
Cat Goes Fiddle-I-Fee
Charlie Needs A Cloak
Down On Grandpa's Farm
Eye Openers - Farm Animals
Farm Animal Book
Farm Noises
Farming
Five Little Ducks
I Went Walking
Mary Had A Little Lamb
Mrs. Wishy Washy
Nine Ducks Nine

Old MacDonald Had A Farm
One Duck Another Duck
Once A Lullaby
Once Upon MacDonald's Farm
Sitting On The Farm
Spots, Feathers and Curly Tails
The Cow That Went Oink
The Farm Concert
The Farmer In The Dell
The Ox-Cart Man
The Year At Maple Hill Farm
There Was An Old Lady Who
   Swallowed A Fly
There's A Hole In The Bucket
Too Much Noise
Wanda The Worm

Class Books & Booklets

Down On Grandpa's Farm
Farm Riddles
First Things First
I Went Walking
Too Much Noise
Where Are The Sheep?

Bingo
Farm Concert
Farmer In The Dell
I Went Walking
One Duck Another Duck
Where's Wanda?

LYN

xi

Songs

Bill Grogan's Goat
Cat Goes Fiddle-I-Fee
Down On Grandpa's Farm
Farmer In The Dell
Five Little Ducks
Mary Had A Little Lamb
Old MacDonald Had A Farm

Once A Lullaby
Sitting On The Farm
There Was An Old Lady Who
   Swallowed A Fly
There's A Hole In The Bucket

Art

All the Make-A-Play Activities
Illustrating Pages for Class Books
Draw With Me Bingo
Old MacDonald Mural
Sticker Wheel Barn
Thumbprint Ducks-Equation Booklet

Science & Math

Animal Sounds
Apple Math
Attaching Quantitative Meaning to Numerals
Attributes & Facts about Farm Animals
Exploring the Production of Wool

Math Equations-One Duck Another Duck
Once Upon MacDonald's Farm 1-10
Scientific Names-Adult, Baby, Male & Female
Sorting & Classifying Farm Pictures of
   Animals, Produce, Machinery, etc.

Drama

 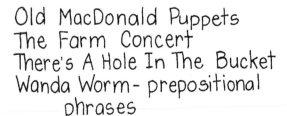

Five Little Ducks
Five Little Ducks Make-A-Play
Mrs. Wishy Washy
Mrs. Wishy Washy Make-A-Play
Old Lady Who Swallowed A Fly
   Make-A-Play

Old MacDonald Puppets
The Farm Concert
There's A Hole In The Bucket
Wanda Worm-prepositional
   phrases

Introduction

EEEEE—HAW!!! Welcome to our farm theme! What fun to visit the farm without having to rise before dawn and collect the eggs, milk the cows and clean out the barn. Just enjoy!

This theme is written in a specific sequence, but it is merely a suggestion. You need not follow this exact order. Choose those activities that best suit your classroom. We are sure that you have many favorites of your own that you will wish to add.

We found it extremely difficult to narrow down our enormous stack of literature for this theme. (Just look at the Bibliography!) Obtaining the materials is quite easy and fun. The difficulty lies in making choices so that we include a variety of teaching strategies.

If you wish to use the big books we have referred to in the text, we suggest you send for them three to four weeks before you plan to begin this theme, as it takes a while for the books to arrive and you will need time to prepare them. The address is as follows:

The Farmer In The Dell
Down On Grandpa's Farm
Whole Language Resources
P.O. Box 426
Hilmar, CA 95324
Phone (209) 668-4142

This theme is meant to be very general in nature. It would be fun to create an in-depth theme on any one of the farm animals and *E-I-E-I-O* would be a great introduction.

We have found the *Come With Me Science Series* to be an excellent resource for many of our themes. *Farm Animals* is one that relates well with *E-I-E-I-O*. If you are interested, the address is: S/S Publishing Co., Rte 1, Box 0180, Shingle Springs, CA 95682.

At the time this book went to press, all the books we have developed were in print. However, books are going in and out of print all the time. If you cannot locate a particular book, try the public library, your school library or contact a local bookstore and they might be able to track the selection down for you.

Happy farming!

Activity 1 — *Old MacDonald Had A Farm*

Materials:

- *Old MacDonald Had A Farm,* by Nancy Hellen
- *Old MacDonald Had A Farm,* by Tracey Campbell Pearson
- *Old MacDonald Had A Farm,* by Tracey English
- *Too Much Noise,* by Ann McGovern
- *Once Upon MacDonald's Farm,* by Stephen Gammell
- Farm animal stickers, four per child
- Brads–one per child
- Blackline 1 for the sticker-wheel barn
- Blackline 2 for the wheel
- Blacklines 3–5 for the pocket chart
  Note: Blackline 5 also contains a picture of *Old MacDonald*
- Ten pieces of 5″ x 6″ tagboard cards to mount pictures from blacklines 3–5
- Blacklines 6–11 for the paper bag puppets
- Blacklines 12–16 for the noun wordbank
- Thirty, 4″ x 5″ tagboard cards to mount the pictures from blacklines 12–16
- Blackline 17 for the class book
- Six lunch-size paper bags for the puppets
- Sentence strips
- Felt pens
- Contact paper or laminating film
- Several colors of butcher paper for a bulletin board mural
- Several colors of construction paper for making bulletin board animals

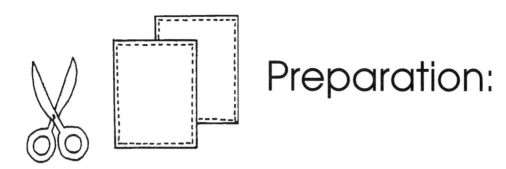

Preparation:

1. Duplicate blackline 1, one per child, on construction paper. You will need to cut the opening as it is too difficult for most 5 and 6 year olds.

2. Duplicate blackline 2, one per child, on white construction paper.

3. Color, cut and mount blacklines 3–5 on 5" x 6" tagboard cards. Contact or laminate. (Refer to *The Old MacDonald* Lift and Look Counting Book by Tracey English)

4. On sentence strips, print the numerals 1–10 and the number words *one* through *ten*. Cut apart into individual word cards. You will also need to print the following on individual word cards:

pig	**cows**	**sheep**
horses	**dogs**	**ducks**
cats	**rabbits**	**mice**
hens		

5. Color, cut and mount blacklines 12–16 on 4" x 5" tagboard cards. Contact or laminate.

6. **For kindergarten:** on sentence strips print the following and cut into individual words: (Cut apart each letter of the E-I-E-I-O line.)

> **Old MacDonald had a farm**
> **E I E I O**
> **And on this farm he had a**
> **E I E I O**

2

You will also need to print on individual word cards the following animal names and sounds: pig, cow, sheep, dog, hen, Old MacDonald, oink, moo, baa, woof, cluck.

7. **For first grade:** on sentence strips print the following and cut into individual words: (Cut apart each letter of the E-I-E-I-O line.)

> **Old MacDonald had a farm, E I E I O.**
> **And on this farm he had a ___, E I E I O.**
> **With a ___ ___ here,**
> **And a ___ ___ there,**
> **Here a ___, there a ___,**
> **Everywhere a ___ ___,**
> **Old MacDonald had a farm, E I E I O.**

Print the following one time only: **pig, cow, sheep, dog, hen**
Print the following two times: **moo, oink, baa, woof, cluck**
Print the following three times: **moo-moo, oink-oink, baa-baa, woof-woof, cluck-cluck**

8. To make paper bag puppets, duplicate one copy each of black-lines 6–11 on the appropriate color of construction paper (pink for the pig. etc.) Use crayons or felt pens to outline and add features to the puppets. Cut and assemble in the following manner:

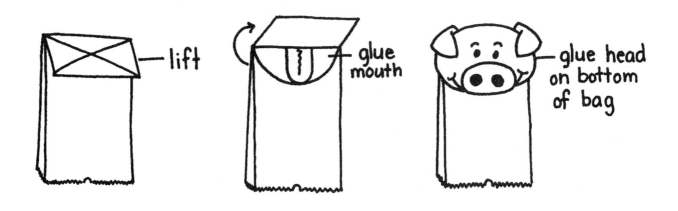

9. Duplicate blackline 17, one per child, for a class book.
10. To prepare for an Old MacDonald mural, staple butcher paper background to your bulletin board. Cut a red barn (enlarge blackline 1 if you wish), a blue pond and a brown mud puddle. You may wish to add a tree and a fence. Label the mural, *Old MacDonald Had A Farm.*

11. The children will have fun making all the animals for the mural. Though we are certain you have many ideas for farm animals, we have included some simple shape animals that are not only fun, but very easy for the children to make. Don't forget to use pink pipe cleaners for the piggies curly tails.

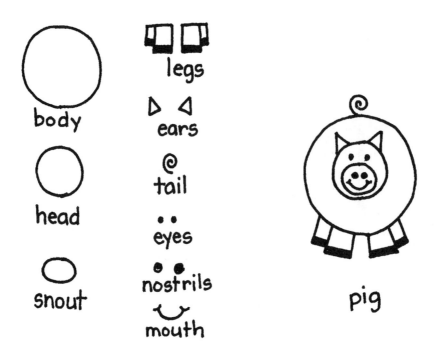

body

head

snout

legs

ears

tail

eyes

nostrils

mouth

pig

12. For the extension, print the following, line-by-line, on sentence strips. Do not cut the words apart.

_____ _____ had a _____. E I E I O

And in this _____ ____ had a _____. E I E I O

With a _____ _____ here and a _____ _____ there,

Here a _____, there a _____,

Everywhere a _____ _____,

_____ _____ had a _____.

E I E I O

Procedure:

1. Show the cover, front and back of Nancy Hellen's book, *Old Mac-Donald Had a Farm*. Ask the children where they would see animals such as these. What would the man be called? Direct their attention to the title at the top of the book.

2. Enjoy singing this clever build-up version of *Old MacDonald*. The children will soon be participating with the repeated phrases.

3. Ask the children to recall the characters in the song. As each one is mentioned, introduce the paper bag puppet. Sing again, letting the children dramatize the song using the puppets. (The build-up format of this story lends itself to this simple drama.) Everyone sings the entire song except for the animal noises. Only the children manipulating the puppets will make those actual sounds.

4. In the pocket chart, place the five animal pictures (found on blacklines 12–16) and Old MacDonald (found on blackline 5), one character per line. Display the cards with the animal names and the animal sounds in another pocket chart, or in a place that is easily accessible to the children. Using phonetic clues, help the children match the names and the sounds to the correct animals. Read or chant. **Note:** Old MacDonald will not have a matching noise. Also, kindergarten may wish only to match the animal names with the pictures.

5. Distribute all the pictures and words to the children, have them find their partners and rebuild in the pocket chart. Read or chant to check for accuracy.

6. **For kindergarten:** Develop the following, line by line, in the pocket chart. Help the children with clues as necessary: What is the first part of the song? How many words are there? Let's clap and count. What do we need first? Now what? etc.

Old		MacDonald		had		a		farm	
E	I	E	I	O					
And		on		this		farm		he		had		a		
E	I	E	I	O					

Sing the song from the pocket chart. Now add the chorus orally *(With a moo-moo here, and a moo-moo there, here a moo, there a moo, everywhere a moo-moo, Old MacDonald had a farm, E I E I O).* Continue in this manner with each additional verse, changing the animal pictures.

7. **For first grade:** Develop the entire song, line by line, in the pocket chart. Help the children with clues as necessary. As each new verse is sung, place the new words and pictures directly on top of the previous ones.

8. Create a noun wordbank by brainstorming on the chalkboard for other things they might encounter on a farm. Chant each of the ideas as they are listed: "On the farm I can see a tractor. On the farm I can see some hay. On the farm I can see an apple tree."

9. A permanent wordbank may be made by using the thirty farm pictures that we have provided. You will want to only use those that your children think of and add to the wordbank as the theme progresses and the children gain more knowledge. Other sources of pictures are color books, National Geographic magazine, calendars, and other children's nature magazines.

10. Read *Old MacDonald Had a Farm,* by Tracey Campbell Pearson. Ask the children to name things that are the same in both selections. Now discuss the things that are different (Farmer's wife, rooster, geese, mule, tractor, cat). Sing the song again creating additional verses with these new characters. By printing the names and noises, these may be added to the pocket chart. The pictures are found in the blackline masters.

11. On a following day, read or sing the book, *Old MacDonald Had a Farm,* by Tracey English. Compare and contrast this new version with the previous two selections.

12. From this discussion it will be obvious that there is a specific number connected with each animal. Help the children place the numeral cards, one through ten, in the pocket chart, being careful to leave room at the left for the number words. Read to check for accuracy. Continue by assisting the children in matching the groups of animals with each numeral. Read again. Next the children match the animal names with the corresponding numerals and animal pictures. Read a third time. Distribute the ten numerals, along with the animal names to the children, leaving the animal pictures in place in the pocket chart. Sing or chant the song again as the children add the words and numerals.

13. Match the corresponding number word to each numeral. (This may be too difficult for many kindergarten and some first grade children.) This offers a great opportunity for working with phonetic clues. Unfortunately, you will have to sing this song one more time! With this last singing, ask the children if they noticed anything different about the rabbit verse.

One	1		pig
Two	2		cows
Three	3		sheep
Four	4		horses
Five	5		dogs
Six	6		ducks
Seven	7		cats
Eight	8		rabbits
Nine	9		mice
Ten	10		hen

Extensions:
Sticker Wheel Song, Old MacDonald Mural and Class Book

Sticker Wheel Song – Distribute blacklines 1–2 to the children. The children need to color the barn. Cut both the barn and the wheel. We suggest that you attach the wheel to the back of barn, matching the dots. Now let the children choose four stickers to place on top of the x's on the wheel. Sing the song, spinning the wheel for each verse. At this point you will want to encourage them to take the song home to sing.

Old MacDonald Mural – Following your own ideas or the samples given, have the children create their individual animals for the mural. The children will enjoy placing these on the bulletin board. At a later date, after the children have learned all the sounds the various animals make, talking bubbles might be added. (See Activity 5.)

Class Book – Read *Too Much Noise,* by Ann McGovern. This is a delightful story not only about farm animal noises but also about everyday ordinary noises. The humor may be a little bit subtle for some kindergarteners, so you may wish to discuss the sequence of events in Peter's house. After reading, brainstorm for things in their own houses that make noise and what the noise would be. List these on the board as they are mentioned.

Place the sentence strips that were prepared in step 12 (Preparation) in the pocket chart. Orally develop eight or ten verses, using the children's first and last names and their choice for the noise. Call attention to he/she if needed.

> **Annie Taylor had a house. E I E I O**
> **And in this house she had a toaster. E I E I O**
> **With a pop pop here and a pop pop there,**
> **Here a pop, there a pop,**
> **Everywhere a pop pop,**
> **Annie Taylor had a house.**
> **E I E I O**

A class book may be created by having each child complete black-line 17. Illustrate and bind. Add this songbook to your class library.

Another musical activity may be experienced by using Raffi's version of *Old MacDonald Had A Band.* It can be sung as is or the names of the instruments changed and dramatized.

For closure, read and enjoy the hilarious *Once Upon MacDonald's Farm,* by Stephen Gammell.

Activity 2 — *I Went Walking*

Materials:

- *I Went Walking,* by Sue Williams (available as a Big Book also)
- *Farm Alphabet Book,* by Jane Miller
- *All About Farm Animals,* by Brenda Cook (or a factual book of your own choice)
- Blacklines 18–19 for the pocket chart
- Seven pieces of 5″ x 6″ tagboard cards to mount the above pictures
- 6″ x 4½″ construction paper in the following colors: black, brown, red, green, pink and yellow
- Blacklines 18–19 (again!) for the individual booklets, each child will need two
- Blackline 20 for the booklet cover
- Blackline 21 for class book page
- Sentence strips
- Felt tip pens
- Contact paper or laminating film
- 9″ x 12″ light blue construction paper for the booklet pages, eight per child
- 9″ x 12″ red construction paper for the booklet covers, two per child
- Tongue blades or popcicle sticks, one per child
- 13″ x 3″ brown or yellow construction paper to make barn roof, one per child
- White strips for barn door trim—each child needs one strip 10½″ x ⅜″ and seven strips that are 8″ x ⅜″

Note: blacklines 18 and 19 will be used once for the pocket chart and two more times for the individual booklets so you will need to make an additional copies of both.

 # Preparation:

1. Make three copies each of blacklines 18–19. Save two sets of blacklines for later. Using the book *I Went Walking* as a reference: color, cut apart and mount one set on 5″ x 6″ tagboard cards. Contact or laminate. These will be used for the pocket chart.

2. Using *I Went Walking* as a guide, print on sentence strips the four repetitive lines beginning with *I went walking*...and ending with ...*at me.* (Copyright prevents us from giving the words to you.) In addition, print the names of the six animals he saw as well as the color words (pink pig, etc.). You will also need to print the last two lines of the book. Cut the entire text into individual word cards.

3. Duplicate blacklines 18–19, two per child, on construction paper. Cut into fourths.

4. Using the text as a guide, make your own blackline of the word strips for this booklet. (Again, copyright prevents us from giving the words to you.) Cut into strips. See the picture under *Extension* for the placement of the strips.

5. Duplicate blackline 20 (the barn door) on red construction paper, one per child.

6. Prepare the brown or yellow barn roof by cutting the 13" x 3" strips as shown below:

Cut on the dotted lines.

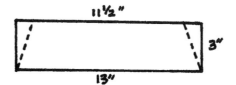

7. To prepare blackline 21, you will need to write in as many or as few words as you choose from the repetitive lines of *I Went Walking.* Duplicate, one per child, for class book pages.
8. Contact or laminate the 6" x 4½" pieces of colored construction paper (black, brown, red, green pink and yellow)

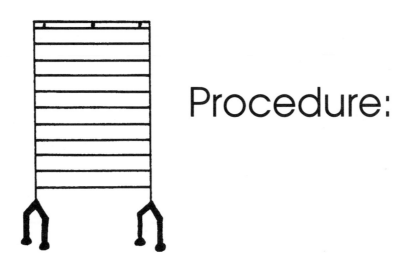

Procedure:

1. Tell the children the name of the book, *I Went Walking,* and show the cover. Ask the children if they have an idea where the little boy is walking. (Where might you see ducks? Where else might you see ducks? Let's find out where this little boy went walking.)
2. Read and enjoy the story, taking time to predict the next animal the little boy will encounter. The children will probably join in on the repetitive parts fairly early. (As the walk progresses, what do the animals do? Elicit from the children that the animals are following the boy.)

3. Read again, having the children join in on the parts that they can chant (Or read if you have the Big Book).
4. Ask the children to recall what animals the little boy saw on his walk. As each one is mentioned, place that picture in the pocket chart. Refer to the book and help the children sequence the animals in the order of the story, placing not only the animal pictures but the 6″ x 4½″ colored construction paper pieces as well.

Using phonetic clues, match the animal names to each picture and then add the color words. (Kindergarten may wish to only use the colored paper instead of color words.) Read to check for accuracy. Distribute all the picture and word cards and let the children find their partners and rebuild this portion in the pocket chart. Read again.
5. Place the repetitive phrase (that was printed in step 2 of the Preparation) in the first four lines of a second pocket chart. Add the remaining words (the last five words of the book, beginning with the word *lot*) to the bottom of the first pocket chart.

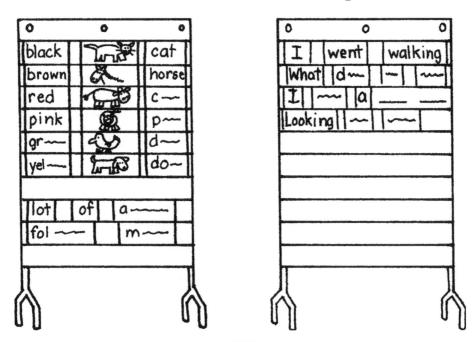

15

To build the entire story, the children will need to complete the sentences in the third and fourth lines of the second pocket chart. They find the correct picture and words and place them in the appropriate spaces. Chant or read. As each new animal is encountered, the children place the new cards and pictures directly on top of the previous ones and chant or read.

Note: The last two words of the story will need to be placed over the last line in the pocket chart.

You may wish to use this question and answer format by having half of the class read the question and the other half read the answer.

6. At this time read and discuss *Farm Alphabet Book*. Refer back to the noun wordbank and chant. Ask the children if there are any other ideas they would like to add to the wordbank. This should give you additional vocabulary for a rewrite of the book, *I Went Walking.*

Extensions: *Class Book and Individual Booklet*

Class Book – Using the structure in the second pocket chart as a guide, help the children orally create new verses by choosing a color word along with an animal (a white lamb, etc.). Be sure to orally develop many verses (at least ten) before attempting the writing portion of this extension.

Each child needs one copy of blackline 21. Using the noun wordbank the children choose one animal and a color for the animal and complete the structure and illustrate. Bind these pages together into a book. Make a cover of your choice, read and add to your class library.

Individual Booklet – This is a copy of the story, *I Went Walking.*
The children will make a stick puppet of themselves and actually
"walk" it through the entire story.

cover   page 1

Cover – Give each child one copy of blackline 20. The barn doors
are created by gluing the white strips along the black lines. (Hint:
we suggest you put the x's on the two doors first and trim off any
excess.) Next, add the sides to the two doors, trimming off any extra. Now add the center strip and trim. Lastly, glue the 10½" x ⅜"
strip along the top line of the two doors. Attach the roof to the top of
the cover, having it extend no more than 1¼" above the top of the
page. The title, **I WENT WALKING**, is printed on the roof.

   Inside the back cover, glue a library pocket near the bottom.
This is where the puppet is stored.

Puppet – Each child needs a copy
of the puppet figure, found on
blackline 18. Children add facial
features and hair. Color the cloth-
ing. Cut the puppet and laminate
as this will strengthen it. Glue the
puppet to a tongue blade or
popcicle stick. Store the puppet in
the library pocket found at the
back of the booklet.

Pages – Each child will need eight pieces of 9″ x 12″ blue construction paper, the text strips that were made in step 4 (Preparation) and two copies of the animals that are found on blacklines 18 and 19. The second copy of the animals will be used for the final page when all the animals are on the path at the same time.

Both sides of the blue construction paper will be used – one side for the question and the other for the answer. To prepare the question pages, the children glue the appropriate words at the top of the paper. Next, encourage the children to use their crayons to create an interesting path for their stick puppet to "walk" along. Grass and flowers may be added. Be sure the children begin their road at the left edge and continue it across the paper to the right edge.

page 2   page 3

For the answer pages, the children repeat all of the above. Next they will need to color and cut the animals. **Note:** The cutting may be a bit difficult for some five- and-six year-olds. We suggest that you draw a bubble around each of the figures before you duplicate them and the children then cut along the bubble line.

18

The animals are now glued to the left side of the path (see illustration). Flowers and grass may be added. You will need two pages for the final answer as it will include all the animals.

Children sequence their pages and the pages are stapled on the left hand side. The children may now walk their puppet through the story as they read.

Activity 3

The Farmer In The Dell

Materials:

- *Farming,* by Gail Gibbons
- *Farm Alphabet Book,* by Jane Miller
- *The Farmer In The Dell,* by Mary Maki Rae
- Blacklines 22–23 for the pocket chart and the accordion book
- Eight 5" x 6" tagboard cards to mount the pocket chart pictures
- Blackline 24 for the accordion book
- Big Book of *The Farmer In The Dell* created by Shirley Handy. This is available from Whole Language Resources, P.O. Box 426, Hilmar, CA 95324, (209) 668-4142.
- Three loose leaf rings for the Big Book
- 18" x 6" pieces of colored construction paper, two per child for the accordion book
- Farm wordbank picture cards from Activity 1 – you will need additional pictures of machinery, personnel, buildings, foods, etc. (Check in color books, magazines, old workbooks, paperback books, etc.)
- Sentence strips
- Felt pens
- Laminating film or contact paper

Preparation:

1. Color and laminate or contact the Big Book. Bind together with three loose leaf rings.

2. For the pocket chart, duplicate one copy of blacklines 22 and 23. Color, cut, mount and laminate. **Note:** you will need blacklines 22 and 23 again for step 4.

3. Print the following words on sentence strips and cut apart into individual word cards: farmer, wife, child, nurse, dog, cat, rat and cheese.

4. Duplicate blacklines 22 and 23, one per child for the accordion book.

5. Duplicate blackline 24, one for every two children, as there are two sets of words on this blackline. Cut in half.

6. To prepare the pages for the accordion book, tape two pieces of 18″ x 6″ strips of construction paper to create one 36″ x 6″ strip. Fold each strip, accordion style, allowing 4½″ for each page. (There will be eight pages when folded.) Each child will need one book.

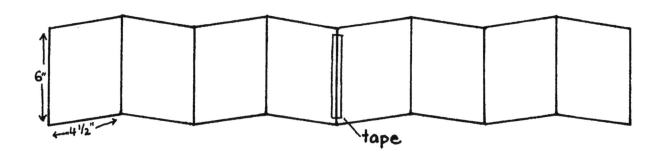

Procedure:

1. Before beginning this activity, you will want to teach your children the words and the drama to the song, *The Farmer in the Dell*. Repeat many times until this becomes familiar. (Your children will love doing this song over and over and over and...)

2. Introduce this lesson by reading and singing either the small paperback version or the Big Book version of *The Farmer in the Dell*, tracking the words with your hands as you go. (You may wish to discuss the meaning of the word *dell*—a small, secluded valley or a glen.)

3. Just for fun, cover the page numbers in the Big Book, remove the loose leaf rings and distribute the pages, at random, to your children. Working together, challenge them to sequence all ten pages of the story. Sing to check for accuracy.

4. Ask the children to name the characters in the song, in the order of appearance—farmer, wife, etc. Place the corresponding pictures in the pocket chart and, using phonetic clues, match the words with the pictures. Read together. Distribute all cards and words to the children. Have them find their partners and rebuild the song in the pocket chart. Sing or read to check for accuracy.

5. The structure of this old favorite is a natural for rewrites—
   we suggest developing the rewrite orally, but of course, some
   children will wish to create their own written versions. Some
   possible ideas for rewrites could include:

   A Christmas rewrite – *Santa's in the room*
   A Halloween rewrite – *A ghost is on the prowl*
   A farm rewrite – *The cow is eating hay*
   A school rewrite – *The principal's out to lunch*

Extensions: *Sorting and Classifying and Accordion Booklet*

Sorting and Classifying – Before beginning any sorting activity,
you will need to develop the vocabulary of the categories and have
reference books available to help answer questions that will occur.
(*Farming* and *Farm Alphabet Book* are two books we like to use.)
We introduce this as a whole group activity using the pocket charts
for the pictures and labels. At a later time, the children work in
cooperative groups creating their own sorting and classifying rules.
The children have great fun challenging the class to guess their rule.

We suggest you begin with things that can be seen on a farm and things you would not see on a farm. Place the labels in the pocket chart and have the children take turns placing the pictures under the appropriate label. Chant the entire sort when it is completed. (A horse is on a farm. A cow is on a farm. An elephant is not on a farm.) Other sorts we could suggest are:

- things that grow and things that don't grow
- has wheels, has legs, has neither wheels nor legs
- is bigger than me, is smaller than me
- by color

Accordion Book – Before beginning this extension, be certain the pictures and word cards from *The Farmer in the Dell* are in the pocket chart. The children may now use these as a reference while they create their individual accordion books.

Each child needs a pre-folded accordion booklet, along with pictures and words from blacklines 22, 23 and 24. They will need to color, cut and mount the pictures, checking with the pocket chart for accuracy. Cut the words and match to the correct pictures. Sing the song together when the booklet is completed.

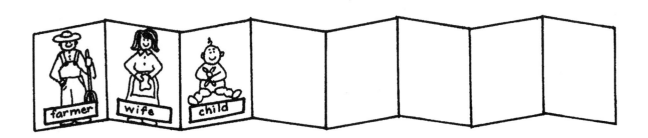

Activity 4

Once A Lullaby

Materials:

- *Once A Lullaby*, by BP Nichol
- *Baby Animals On The Farm*, by Hans-Heinrich Isenbart, or any reference book dealing with adult and baby farm animals. (We are told that this book is out of print at this time. We recommend you check the library since it was a School Library Journal *BEST BOOK OF THE YEAR, 1983.)*
- *Eye Openers—Farm Animals* (a reference book that is in print)
- *Build A Doodle Farm*, by Beverly Armstrong (a step-by-step drawing book)
- *Spot Goes to the Farm*, by Eric Hill
- Blacklines 25–31 for the pocket chart
- Twenty-eight 5″ x 6″ tagboard cards to mount the above pictures
- Blackline 32 for the class book
- Sentence strips
- Felt pens
- Laminating film or contact paper

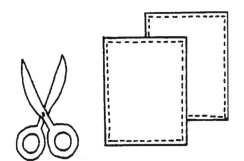

Preparation:

1. For the pocket chart, duplicate one copy of blacklines 25–31. Color, cut, mount on tagboard cards and laminate.
   Note: Save the original blacklines as you may wish to use these at a later date.

2. On sentence strips, print the following and cut into individual word cards:

horse	foal	donkey	foal
cow	calf	pig	piglet
goat	kid	sheep	lamb
hen	chick	duck	duckling
goose	gosling	turkey	chick
dog	puppy	cat	kitten
rabbit	bunny	owl	owlet

3. On sentence strips, print the following:

   First things first.
   First a _____ , then a _____ .
   First things first.

4. Duplicate blackline 32, one per child, for the class book.

Procedure:

1. Read or sing the book, *Once A Lullaby.* (**Note:** the melody is found at the back of the book.) The wonderful illustrations and the simplicity along with the repetition will soon make this one of your classroom favorites.

2. Though the pages are small, the illustrations need to be developed. At the present time, this enchanting book is available in paperback for approximately $5.00. It might be worth having three or four copies so the children are able to break into small groups to examine and read this book.

   Begin by asking, "What do you notice?" Continue until the children have examined the entire illustration. You will want to include in your discussion the family portrait, the pictures on the headboard and footboard, the picture frame, the legs on bed, the coverlet on the bed, the toy, the books, the wallpaper and the occupants of the bed. Be sure to include the two small pictures on either side of the text.

3. Help the children compare the similarities and differences in all the illustrations. Read the book again, with the children participating.

4. Because this book talks about baby animals, it is a perfect lead into a lesson about the adult and the baby animals that live on a farm. Ask the children to name all the farm animals they can think of, using the noun wordbank as a reference. As each ani-

mal is named, place the picture of that particular animal on the left side of the pocket chart. (You will need two pocket charts to fit the fourteen animals we have given you.) The children now chant each animal: "This is a cow. This is a horse." etc.

5. Using a reference book of your choice (We like *Baby Animals On The Farm* or the book, *Eye Openers—Farm Animals*) help the children name the adult animals. You may wish to use the general animal name such as horse, or the appropriate male and female adult names, such as stallion or mare. In the preparation of this lesson you printed the general animal names. If you wish to go into more detail, you will need to print the other names as well.

The following information may be helpful with this lesson:

ANIMAL	MALE	FEMALE	YOUNG
horse	stallion	mare	foal
donkey	jack	jenny	jennet
cow	bull	cow	calf
pig	boar	sow	piglet
goat	billy	nanny	kid
sheep	ram	ewe	lamb
chicken	rooster	hen	chick
duck	drake	duck	duckling
goose	gander	goose	gosling
turkey	tom	hen	chick
dog	dog	dog	puppy
cat	tom	queen	kitten
rabbit	buck	doe	bunny
owl	owl	owl	owlet

6. Place the pictures of the baby animals in the bottom of the second pocket chart. Help the children match the adult with the baby. Place the baby animal picture next to the adult animal picture, leaving room for the word cards (see illustration). Chant "This is a pig. This is a piglet" etc.

7. Using phonetic clues, the children now match the appropriate words with each picture. Read.

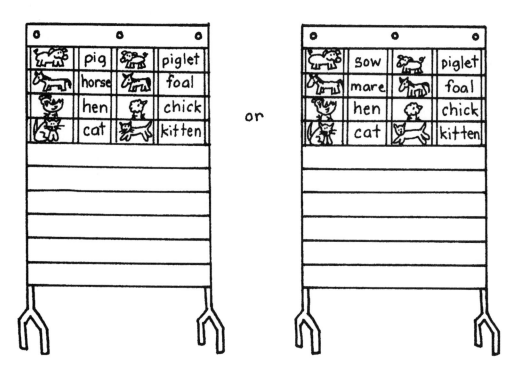

or

8. Either distribute all pictures or all words to the children. Rebuild in the pocket chart. Read to check for accuracy.

 Extension: *First Things First Class Book*

1. Place in the pocket chart the frame you printed in step 3 under Preparation.
2. The children take turns picking a baby and adult animal. They place the pictures or words in the frame and read:

   "First things first.
   First a piglet, then a pig.
   First things first."

3. Prior to making the class booklet, you may wish to spend some time with directed drawing of the farm animals, using *Build A Doodle Farm* as a guide.

   Distribute blackline 32 to the children, one per child. Each child chooses an animal and, using the pocket chart as a guide, completes the frame. They then illustrate with the adult and the baby animal. Bind these pages into a class booklet, add a cover and put it in your library.

   Note: You might wish to have the children work in partners so that one child illustrates the adult animal and the other child illustrates the baby.
4. For closure, the children enjoy *Spot Goes To The Farm*, where Spot encounters many of the baby animals they have just learned about.

Activity 5

The Farm Concert

Materials:

- *The Farm Concert,* by Joy Cowley (This book is distributed by the Wright Group and is available in Big Book format or in a smaller version that comes in packets of six.)
- *The Cow That Went Oink,* by Bernard Most
- *Farm Noises,* by Jane Miller
- Sentence strips
- Chart paper
- Blackline 33 for the pocket chart
- Six pieces of 4″ x 5″ tagboard cards to mount the above pictures
- 9″ x 6″ construction paper for individual booklet covers, two per child
- Farm animal stickers, six different animals per child
- Felt pens
- Laminating film or contact paper

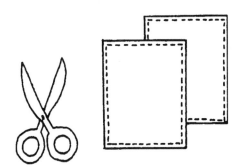

Preparation:

1. Duplicate blackline 33. Color, cut and mount on tagboard cards. Laminate or contact.

2. The first step in preparing for the individual booklets is to obtain farm animal stickers. We do not limit the animals to only those in the book, *The Farm Concert*. (It's often difficult to find a frog and a dog, so we opt for more farm animals such as a rooster and a goat.)

   Another option is to use stamps, rather than stickers. These are found in catalogs, stores that carry educational supplies or in specialty shops.

   To prepare for the individual booklets, you will need to make your own blacklines. You may wish to give the children all the words, some of the words or have the children write the entire page. Depending on your class, make the blacklines and duplicate enough pages for your children.

We find it is easier to assemble these booklets before they are used in the extension activity. Therefore, you will need to staple the pages, along with the cover, one booklet per child.

3. On sentence strips, print the following names and noises and cut into individual word cards:

cow	Moo, moo
frog	Croak, croak
pig	Oink, oink
duck	Quack, quack
dog	Wuff, wuff
sheep	Baa, baa

4. Depending upon the stickers or stamps you have chosen, prepare the six sentences you will use in your booklet by printing each one on a separate strip. Add an appropriate sticker at the end of each strip.

   "Neigh, neigh," went the horse. (sticker)
   "Cluck, cluck," went the hen. (sticker)
   etc.

5. On chart paper, print the following:

   The Big Red Barn

   When the farmer's day is done,
   In the barnyard, every one,
   The cow says, "MOO!"
   The pigeon, "COO!"
   The sheep says, "BAA!"
   The lamb says, "MAA!"
   The hen, "CLUCK, CLUCK!"
   "QUACK!" says the duck;
   The dog, "BOW-WOW!"
   The cat, "MEOW!"
   The horse says, "NEIGH!
   I love sweet hay!"
   Then the farmer says, "GOODNIGHT!"
   And locks the big red barn up tight.

   Author Unknown

If you have any left over stickers, they are an added treat to this poem.

6. Print the following poem on sentence strips:

I went to visit a farm one day
I saw a _____ across the way
And what do you think I heard it say?

_____ _____ _____

Procedure:

1. Discuss the cover of *The Farm Concert*. Tell the children the title of the book and ask them if they know what a concert is. Develop the meaning of concert (musical performance) and elicit from the children the animals are putting on this concert. Help the children name the animals and predict how that animal would sing.
2. Read the book, taking time to discuss the pictures on each page. The children will immediately be able to predict what happens next. Call the children's attention to the change in print size as well as to the " " *talking marks*.
3. Read, my turn, your turn.
4. Help the children sequence the animal pictures in the pocket chart. Refer to the book to check for accuracy. Using phonetic

clues, match the animal name with the animal picture and read. Now, using phonetic clues again, match the animal sounds. Read.

5. Distribute all the picture and word cards to the children. They find their partners and rebuild the story in the pocket chart. Read to check for accuracy.

6. This is a must for dramatization! There are several ways to develop this. One way is to divide your class into six groups, each group taking the part of one animal and the teacher taking the part of the farmer. To get a real feel for the noise this concert produced, have each group continue repeating their part as the new group is added.

   Another way to develop this story is for individual children to take the parts of the animals. Be sure to dramatize enough times to ensure each child has a chance to participate.

   And one of our favorites is all the children take all the parts—noisy but so very fun!

   From the dramatization, it will be easy for the children to contrast the two concerts the animals gave.

7. Introduce the book *Farm Noises*. As you read, have the children join in with the animal noises. Discuss which animals were in this book that weren't in *The Farm Concert*.

8. Read the poem, *The Big Red Barn* (that was printed on chart paper). The children will immediately be able to join in with the animal sounds. This is a fun poem to have a narrator and a chorus, with the teacher initially taking the part of the narrator and the entire class the chorus. (The chorus reads everything in quotation marks.)

Extension: *Individual Sticker Booklets*

1. Place the sentence strips you prepared in step 4 under Preparation, in the pocket chart, one strip at a time. Referring to the sticker at the end of the sentence strip, ask the children to name the animal and tell the sound that it makes. Read the strip together ("Quack, quack," said the duck.) etc.

2. Distribute the pre-assembled booklets, along with the stickers you chose. The children use the sentences in the pocket chart as a reference to complete the writing in the booklets. Lastly, add the sticker (or stamp).

3. The children write *The Farm Concert* on the cover of their booklet. The booklets can be read as a group or with a partner.

4. In the pocket chart place the poem that was printed in step 6 under Preparation. In a second pocket chart, place all the animal pictures, animal names and the sounds.

     The children take turns choosing an animal and placing the appropriate picture and words in the blank spaces of the poem. Read together.

5. Read the book, *The Cow That Went Oink*, by Bernard Most. This hilarious book not only deals with animal sounds but also with human nature. It is especially nice to read with ESL children. Learning a new language is a difficult task, as the cow and pig discover.

Note: At this time you may wish to make a talking bubble for each animal on the mural that was made in Activity 1.
It is fun to see the children "reading" the bulletin boards!

Activity 6

Five Little Ducks

Materials:

- *Five Little Ducks*, by Jose Aruego and Ariane Dewey
- *One Duck, Another Duck*, by Charlotte Pomerantz
- *Nine Ducks Nine*, by Sarah Hayes
- 18" x 4" light blue construction paper for the extension booklets (lots)
- 12" x 18" light blue constructiion paper for make-a-play folder, one per child
- Blackline 34 of clouds for the extension booklets
- Blackline 35 for the booklet covers
- Blacklines 36-37 for make-a-play
- Blackline 38 of the water for the make-a-play
- Blackline 39-40 for the pocket chart
- Eight pieces of 4" x 5" tagboard to mount the pictures of the eight baby ducks
- Two pieces of 5" x 6" tagboard to mount the pictures of the two adult ducks
- Some type of manipulative for equation work
- Stamp pads
- Sentence strips
- Contact paper or laminating film

Preparation:

Make-a-play

1. Duplicate blackline 38 on dark blue construction paper.
   Note: Cut on the dotted line to separate the two sections of water. Each child will need only one section.
2. Fold the 12" x 18" light blue construction paper in half so it measures 9" x 12", one per chlld.
3. Duplicate blacklines 36–37 of the ducks, one set of characters per child. Cut apart on the bold lines.

Pocket Chart

4. Duplicate blacklines 39–40. Color, cut and mount on tagboard cards. (eight pieces of 4" x 5" and two pieces of 5" x 6') Contact or laminate.
5. On sentence strips print the numerals 1–10, a second numeral one (1) card, two plus (+) signs and an equal (=) sign. Cut these apart and laminate or contact.

Extension Booklet

6. Duplicate blackline 34 of the clouds on white construction paper. These will be used, one cloud per page, in the extension booklet. The children will write one equation on each cloud. Use one or two pages of clouds per student, depending upon the amount of equations the child will be completing. Younger children may only wish to do five. Please note that one of the clouds contains the title and will be used on the cover.

7. Duplicate blackline 35 on manila construction paper. Cut in half. Each child will need one copy of Grandmother and Danny for the cover of the booklet.

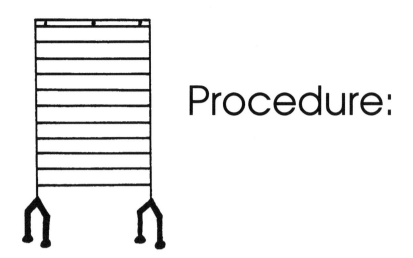

Procedure:

1. Sing or read *Five Little Ducks*. If you are singing, be sure to sing the last verse (Sad Mother Duck...) very slowly and sadly. It took us many singings and readings of this great story before we noticed the subtleties in the pictures. Help the children discover the changing seasons (almost a year has passed) and the return of the five little ducks with their new families. Now we know where they went! Mother duck now has fifteen little grandducks. The children will also enjoy the patterns, both in color and in number on the last page.

2. This story is a must for drama. Let the five little ducks choose a place in the classroom to hide as they leave the mother duck. This is so popular that you will sing and dramatize for days on end. Each child will have many turns before they grow tired!

3. So that the children will be able to retell the story at home, we like to make-a-play. Begin with the water. This will be both one of the backdrops as well as a storage area for all the characters of this play. Cut the dark blue water (blackline 38). Open up the large 12″ x 18″ light blue construction paper folder. If you open the folder, the children are less apt to try to glue the water upside

down! Carefully glue around the sides and bottom of the water, being sure not to glue the top. Glue the water to the paper folder, matching the corners at the bottom. You have now created a storage pocket. Using crayons, have the children illustrate clouds and a sun at the top.

4. Have the children turn the opened folder around and illustrate and the color the hills, the sun and the clouds.

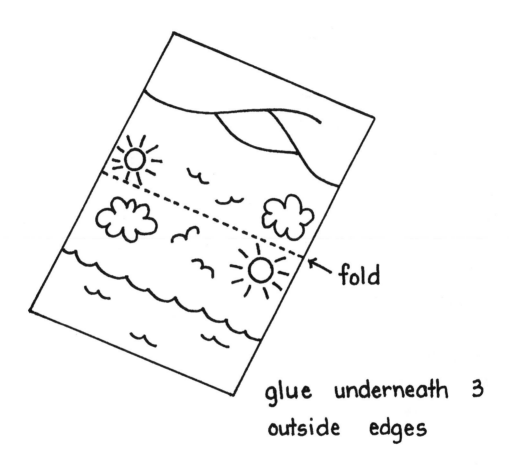

glue underneath 3 outside edges

5. Color the mother duck and five little ducks from blacklines 39–40. Carefully fold on the dotted lines. Be sure to tell your children not to cut the individual ducks as they do not stand as well as the larger rectangles.

6. When completed, stand up the folder and place the characters to one side of the folder. Now the children are ready to retell the story, using the characters to dramatize the action—thus, making-a-play. Before taking home, have the children place all of the characters in the pocket behind the water and close the folder.

1. Read and enjoy the book, *One Duck, Another Duck.* After the first reading, ask the children if they can think of another way to describe the action as each new duck is spotted. How would the mathematician say it?
2. Give each child a paper plate (or a napkin, blue construction paper, etc.) and ten manipulatives such as duck crackers, macaroni, beans, unifix cubes, etc.
3. Reread the first equation, which appears on pages 6–7 in the book. Have the children create this equation with their duck crackers. The children chant the equation and count on to arrive at the answer (1 + 1 = 2).

Pocket Chart

4. Help the children build this equation in the pocket chart with the duck pictures and numeral cards.

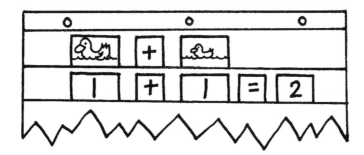

5. Be sure to remove all the cards after each equation as we want the children to focus on only one equation at a time. Also, we have not provided you with enough ducks to have all ten equations showing at one time.
6. Continue, following steps 3 and 4, with each new equation.

Booklet

7. To make the cover, each child will need a copy of blackline 35, a cloud with the title printed on it, and one piece of 18" x 4" light blue construction paper. The children color and cut Grandmother and Danny. On the construction paper, draw a limb on which the owls will sit. Glue down the owls. Last of all add the cloud title.

8. Before beginning the booklet, glue a white cloud at the top of each page. Every child will build the equations with their crackers and record them on the white clouds (one equation per page). Be certain to build and record all the equations before illustrating.

9. Illustrations for each page are made by creating thumbprint ducks. These need to be created so that there are distinct groupings to represent each equation that is recorded. We suggest using ink pads, however, tempra will also work. It is much easier to have the children make all the thumbprints for the entire booklet at one time. After the ink or tempra has dried, the children use fine line felt pens to add details.

When completed, the children may wish to read their equations to a friend.

10. For closure read *Nine Ducks Nine* and enjoy the humor.

Activity 7

Mary Had A Little Lamb

Materials:

- *Mary Had A Little Lamb,* photo-illustrated by Bruce McMillan
- *Charlie Needs A Cloak,* by Tomie de Paola
- Factual book with reference to lambs
- Sentence strips
- Blacklines 41–43 for the pocket chart pictures to *Mary Had A Little Lamb* and *Little Bo Peep*
- Eleven pieces of 5" x 6" tagboard cards to mount the above pictures
- Blackline 44 for the pocket chart and for individual accordion books
- Five pieces of 4" x 4" tagboard to mount the above pictures
- 6" x 24" strip of construction paper, one per child, for the accordion book
- Blacklines 45–46 for the sheep facts booklet
- Cotton balls
- Two large pieces of butcher paper
- Laminating film or contact paper

Preparation:

1. Duplicate blacklines 41–43 for the pocket chart. Color, cut and mount on 5″ x 6″ tagboard cards. Contact or laminate.

2. **Note:** You will be using blacklines 44 and 45 two times. Duplicate blackline 44. Color, cut and mount on 4″ x 4″ tagboard cards. Laminate or Contact. Duplicate blackline 44 again, this time one per child.

3. Duplicate blackline 45 on white construction paper, two per child. These circles will be used for the front and back covers to the individual booklets.

4. Duplicate blackline 45 once more, on ditto paper, approximately 4–6 per child. (See extension for suggestions for kindergarten) These will be used for the booklet pages.

5. Duplicate blackline 46, one per two children, on white construction paper. These will be used on the cover for the booklet.

6. Accordion fold the 6″ x 24″ construction paper strips into five equal spaces to be used for the accordion book.

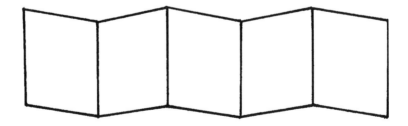

7. On the top of two large pieces of butcher paper print:

Where did Little Bo Peep's sheep go?
What was Bo Peep doing when the sheep disappeared?

8. On sentence strips print the numerals 1–5 and the following words:

shear   card   spin   weave   sew

Cut apart into individual word cards and laminate or contact.

9. On sentence strips, print the following:
(Each line will go with each of the six pocket chart pictures)

Mary had a little lamb, its fleece was white as snow.
And everywhere that Mary went the lamb was sure to go.
It followed her to school one day. That was against the rule.
It made the children laugh and play to see a lamb at school.
And so, the teacher turned it out, but still it lingered near;
And waited patiently about, till Mary did appear.

10. On sentence strips, print the following:
(one line for each picture)

Little Bo Peep
Has lost her sheep,
And doesn't know where to find them;
Leave them alone and they'll come home,
Wagging their tails behind them.

Procedure:

1. **Note:** Before beginning this activity, you will want to familiarize yourself with the information found on the last three pages in *Mary Had A Little Lamb*. We found this really fascinating!

   Introduce this lesson by singing or reading from the book, *Mary Had a Little Lamb*. Sing or chant several times until the children are familiar with it. (Please note that we will only be using a portion of this poem in the pocket chart.)

2. Chant again, placing the pictures from blacklines 41–42 in the pocket chart, one picture per line. Add the words, one line at a time, tracking and reading as you proceed.

3. Tell the children we are going to work with another nursery rhyme, only this time the lamb is grown up. Ask the children what we call this animal. There is a little girl in this nursery rhyme as well, only her name is Bo Peep – and she, like Mary, has a problem.

   Chant the nursery rhyme, *Little Bo Peep,* until the children have it memorized.

4. Chant again, placing the pictures from blacklines 42–43 in the pocket chart, one picture per line.

5. Add the words, one line at a time, tracking as you go. First grade children will be able to match the phrases to the pictures with little help.

47

6. At this point you might want to ask the children where they think Bo Peep's sheep could possibly have gone. Record the children's responses on the large piece of butcher paper, using both pictures and words. Some responses might include in the meadow, under the bridge, over the hill, behind the barn, etc. (Some of our favorites from past years are: at Las Vegas, on the school bus, taking a nap, at the zoo visiting their friends, at the roller rink and at McDonalds eating french fries.) Chant each of the responses several times – The sheep are _____ .

7. On another day, review the poem and ask the children what they think Bo Peep was doing when the sheep disappeared. Was she paying attention? Again, record the children's responses on butcher paper, using both illustrations and print. Chant the brainstorming – Bo Peep was _____ .

Both steps 6 and 7 can be easily adapted as class books. The children refer to the brainstorming on the butcher paper and illustrate on their individual papers. You may wish to write the words or have the children copy from the butcher paper. Bind when completed.

8. Ask the children to tell you what facts they know about lambs. Record these on the chalkboard. Read any factual books you have about lambs. Discuss this information and review what the children initially listed. Are there any facts that need to be altered or revised? Some questions you might wish to consider include Where do lambs live? What do lambs eat? How do lambs communicate? How big are lambs, and how long do they live? What is a lamb's family like?

Extensions: *Lamb Shape Book and Accordion Book*

Lamb Shape Book

Before duplicating blackline 45 for kindergarten, you may wish to prepare the pages in the following manner:

To prepare the booklets, complete the following:

Front cover – Each child needs one copy of blacklines 45–46 that have been duplicated on construction paper. Cut one round body shape and the head. Add crayon features to the head. Cover the body with cotton balls. Set the head aside for now.

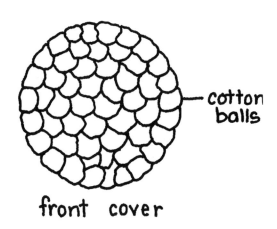

front cover

Back cover – Each child needs one copy of blacklines 45–46. Color the legs black and cut. Then cut the round body shape. Glue the legs to the bottom of the body shape.

back cover

Have the children cut 4–6 pages for their book. (Each page is just a round body shape from blackline 45.) Staple the pages between the front and back cover at the top.

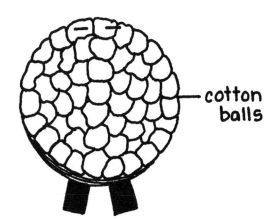

cotton balls

The children choose one fact from the brainstorming to write on each page and illustrate. After completing their stapled booklet, the head may be glued to the front cover.

cotton balls

Accordion Book

1. Discuss what your class knows about processing material.
2. To develop the content area, tell the children you will be asking them to tell you all the things they can remember from the book you are about to read.
3. Read *Charlie Needs A Cloak.*
4. Brainstorm on the board for all the procedures they remember from the book.
5. Ask what tools were used. Put the pictures of the tools in the pocket chart as the children name them.
6. Put the numerals 1–5 in the pocket chart and, using the book as a reference, sequence the pictures to match the numerals.

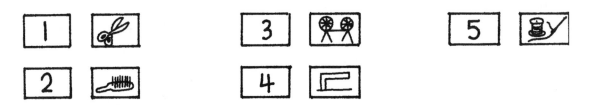

7. Discuss how each tool is used and add the appropriate word.

8. Chant, "First we shear; second we card..."
9. Each child cuts apart pictures, words and numerals from blackline 44. These are glued down in the correct order on the accordion folder paper.

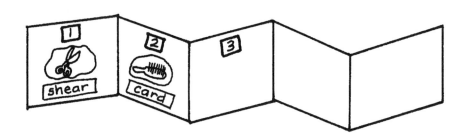

10. Invite a spinner or weaver to come to the classroom to share his or her expertise.

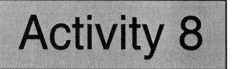

Activity 8

Down On Grandpa's Farm

Materials:

- *Farming,* by Gail Gibbons
- *The Year At Maple Hill Farm,* by Alice and Martin Provensen
- *Ox-Cart Man,* by Donald Hall
- *Down On Grandpa's Farm,* big book distributed by The Singing-Reading Connection (P.O. Box 426, Hilmar, CA 95324)
- *Down On Grandpa's Farm,* TRC Song Strips (P.O. Box 1509, San Leandro, CA 94577)
- *Down On Grandpa's Farm,* TRC Song Tape (optional)
- Blackline 47 for the pocket chart
- Five pieces of 4" x 6" tagboard cards to mount the above pictures
- Blackline 48 for the class book
- Picture cards from the noun wordbank (see Activity 1)
- Wintergreen peppermint candies, one per child
- Sentence strips
- Laminating film or contact paper

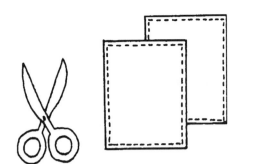

Preparation:

1. Duplicate blackline 47. Color, cut and mount on tagboard cards. (Please note that the color of each animal is mentioned in the big book.) Contact or laminate.

2. Duplicate blackline 48, one per child, for the class book.

3. On sentence strips, print the following and cut apart into word cards:

a big brown cow	**Moo! Moo!**
a little red hen	**Cluck! Cluck!**
a little white sheep	**Baa! Baa!**
a big black dog	**Woof! Woof!**
a big brown horse	**Neigh! Neigh!**

4. Color and laminate or contact the big book, *Down On Grandpa's Farm.*

Procedure:

1. Introduce the song *Down On Grandpa's Farm* with the big book. Track the words as you sing, encouraging the children to join in as soon as they are able – which will be soon, with all the repetition! (Be sure to take time to have the children predict what sound each animal will make.)

2. Sing the song again, in an echo manner. Divide your class in two groups. On each animal page, the groups will alternate singing the lines. On the refrain (Oh, we're on our way...) everybody sings.

3. You will find many valuable suggestions for developing the song in the pocket chart in the TRC Song Strip Guide. The directions are self-explanatory.

    However, if you teach younger children, you may wish to work with fewer words and develop the song in the following way. Help the class to sequence the animal pictures in the pocket chart. Then using phonetic clues, the children match the words with the appropriate picture. Lastly, add all the animal sounds. Sing or read. Now distribute all the word cards and pictures. The children then rebuild the song in the pocket chart, verse by verse. Sing to check for accuracy.

Referring to the noun wordbank, sing the song again and again, each time having the children choose something new from Grandpa's farm (a big red tractor – vroooom, vroooom). This song is an ideal introduction into the workings of a real farm.

4. Read and discuss *Farming,* by Gail Gibbons. This is an excellent overall introduction to farming. Some vocabulary that you may wish to develop include the following: grains, chicken house, patch, planter, pasture, maple syrup, fertilized, plowed, harrowed, chores, care, nectar, hoe, mower, bale, tedder, raker, vet, hayloft, frost, silo, harvested, market, dairy, bushels, bare, machinery, poultry. From this discussion, your class will be able to add new ideas to the noun wordbank.

   Another good resource is *The Year At Maple Hill Farm,* by Alice and Martin Provensen. For older children, you may wish to read both factual books.

5. On another day, introduce and read the old favorite, *Ox-Cart Man,* by Donald Hall. Some words that may need to be developed include the following: flax, shingles, birch brooms, split, carved, barrel, honeycomb, maple sugar, tapped, sap, goose feathers, villages, shawl, ox cart, ox, wintergreen peppermint candies, iron kettle, yoke, harness, embroidery needle, stitching, whittling, planks.

   Whenever possible bring in the actual items mentioned in the story. The experience will be much more meaningful as the children touch and investigate each object.

6. At the end of the story give each child a wintergreen peppermint candy to enjoy. This would be a good time to compare and contrast the workings of farms of today and the farm mentioned in *Ox-Cart Man.* For older children, these can be listed on two separate sheets of butcher paper. They could be titled *Farms of Yesterday and Farms of Today.* This would be a good time to include some independent writing.

Extension: *Class Book*

Sing *Down On Grandpa's Farm* again, creating new verses from the newly acquired information. Distribute blackline 48, one per child. The children, referring to the noun wordbank, choose something that would be on Grandpa's Farm. This word is used to complete the sentence and then the page is illustrated. Add a cover, bind together into a class book and sing!

Activity 9

Mrs. Wishy Washy

Materials:

- *Mrs. Wishy Washy,* by Joy Cowley and June Melser (the big book version, if possible)
- *Cat Goes Fiddle-i fee,* by Paul Galdone
- Blacklines 49–51 for *Mrs. Wishy Washy* make-a-play
- Blacklines 52–64 for Bill Grogan's *Goat* big book
- 12" x 18" construction paper, one per child, for the make-a-play cover
- Sixteen pieces of 12" x 18" construction paper for the big book pages
- 6" x 9" brown construction paper for the make-a-play
- Sentence strips
- Large wash tub and scrub brush (optional)
- Laminating film or contact paper

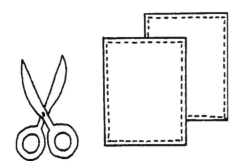

Preparation:

1. Duplicate blacklines 49–51 on construction paper, one per child, for the make-a-play. Cut the characters apart on the solid line. (The dotted line will be used as a fold line.)

2. Fold in half any color of 12″ x 18″ construction paper so it measures 9″ x 12″, one per child, for the make-a-play cover.

3. Duplicate blacklines 52–64 for the big book.

4. For the big book, color blacklines 52–64. Print two copies of the text with felt pens on sentence strips. Print one set in one color and the second set (echo) in a corresponding color. Text is as follows:

> **Bill Grogan's goat**
> **Was feeling fine,**
> **Ate three red shirts**
> **From off the line.**
>
> **Bill took a stick,**
> **Gave him a whack**
> **And tied him to**
> **The railroad track.**
>
> **The whistle blew,**
> **The train drew nigh,**
> **Bill Grogan's goat**
> **Was doomed to die.**
>
> **He gave three groans**
> **Of awful pain,**
> **Coughed up the shirts**
> **And flagged the train!**

5. Glue each picture and the corresponding sentence strips on 12" x 18" construction paper as shown.

Bill Grogan's goat

Bill Grogan's goat

page 1

Was feeling fine,

Was feeling fine,

page 2

Ate three red shirts

Ate three red shirts

page 3

From off the line.

From off the line.

page 4

Bill took a stick

Bill took a stick

page 5

Gave him a whack

Gave him a whack

page 6

And tied him to

And tied him to

page 7

The railroad track.

The railroad track.

page 8

The whistle blew,

The whistle blew,

page 9

The train drew nigh,

The train drew nigh,

page 10

Bill Grogan's goat

Bill Grogan's goat

page 11

Was doomed to die.

Here lies Bill Grogan's Goat Met a train! June 5, 1900

Was doomed to die.

page 12

He gave three groans

ooh!

ooh!

OOH!

He gave three groans

page 13

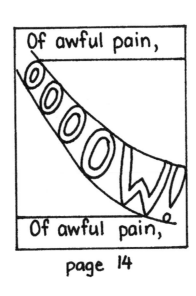

Of awful pain,

OOOOOW!

Of awful pain,

page 14

Coughed up the shirts

Coughed up the shirts

page 15

6. **Note:** You will need to illustrate pages 13 and 14 with groans of pain.
7. Laminate or contact and bind with loose leaf rings.

And flagged the train!

And flagged the train!

page 16

60

Procedure:

1. Show the children the cover of the book, *Mrs. Wish Washy*. Ask them why they think she is wearing an apron. What do you think she is going to wash?

2. Read Mrs. Wishy Washy, using the big book version if possible. There are many opportunities for the children to predict what the animals will do and what Mrs. Wishy Washy will do.

3. Have the children demonstrate the actions for jumped, rolled and paddled. Discuss why the animals think mud is lovely.

4. To prepare for dramatization, discuss how the animals would say, "Oh, lovely mud!" and how Mrs. Wishy Washy would say, "Just look at you!" and "In the tub you go!"

5. Reread, having the children join in. The children will pick up the meter and words very quickly. Now divide your class into four groups. (Mrs. Wishy Washy, the cow, the pig, the duck) Read again, this time having the groups read their parts. The teacher may need to be the narrator with younger children.

6. Dramatize, with the children retelling the story. All the children will act out all the parts during the first dramatization. Use the book as a reference, if needed.

7. Allow the children, four at a time, to act out the parts of Mrs. Wishy Washy, the cow, the pig and the duck. If you have a large tub and scrub brush, it adds to the fun! Be sure to repeat the performances until all the children have had a turn.

8. Tell the children you have a song about another problem with animals. This time the animal is a goat. He is owned by a man named Bill Grogan. Introduce this song using the big book. Sing and track through the first reading.

9. Sing again, using my turn, your turn (echo), with the teacher singing the first line, and the children singing the repeated line. After the children know the song, divide the class in half and sing with one half singing the top line and the second half singing the bottom line.

Extension: *Make a play*

1. Every child needs one copy of each of the characters and the wash tub from blacklines 49–51. They also need one piece of 6″ x 9″ brown construction paper for the mud puddle and one piece of folded 12″ x 18″ construction paper for the cover.

2. The children color blacklines 49–51. The characters are folded on the dotted lines. We do not recommend cutting the characters as they stand better as rectangles.

3. The tub is cut out and glued to the right side of the folded construction paper. The mud is cut from the brown construction paper and is glued to the left side.

4. Print Mrs. Wishy Washy on the front cover.
5. When completed, the children can retell the story, using the characters to dramatize the action.

6. A delightful book (song) for closure is *The Cat Goes Fiddle-i-fee.*

Activity 10 *BINGO*

Materials:

- *There's A Hole in the Bucket,* illustrated by Nadine Bernard Westcott
- Blacklines 65–66 for the pocket chart
- Seven pieces of 5″ x 6″ tagboard cards to mount the above blacklines
- Blacklines 67–68 for the pocket chart and for the extension booklets
- Fifteen pieces of 4″ x 5″ tagboard cards to mount the above pictures
- Contact paper or laminating film
- 12″ x 18″ light colored construction paper, one per child, for the extension booklet
- *Build a Doodle Farm,* by Beverly Armstrong (optional)
- *Ed Emberley's Drawing Book of Animals,* by Ed Emberly (optional)
- Sentence strips

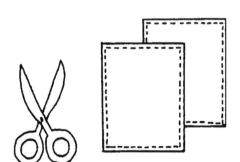

Preparation:

1. Duplicate one copy of blacklines 65–66. Color, cut and mount on tagboard cards. Laminate or contact.
2. Duplicate three copies of blacklines 67. Set the three handclapping pictures aside (See step 3). Color, cut and mount on 4″ x 5″ tagboard cards.

3. Duplicate two copies blackline
   67. Color and cut the fifteen
   hand-clapping circles (be sure
   to include the three from
   blackline 66). Mount these on
   the back of the letter cards,
   one circle per card.

front   **back**

4. For the extension booklet, each child will need one set of letters
   (blackline 66) and five handclapping circles. Duplicate these on
   white construction paper.

5. On sentence strips, print the following:

   There was a farmer
   Had a dog
   And Bingo was his name-o
   And Bingo was his name-o

Cut the above into individual word cards.

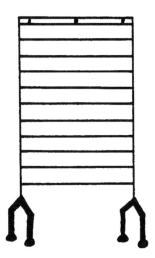

1. Introduce this activity by singing the book, *There's a Hole in the
   Bucket.* (**Note:** the melody is on the last page of the book.)
2. Discuss each page in the book, calling attention to the humor the
   artist has so cleverly depicted. You will want to begin looking at
   the pictures on the title page to help the children understand

why Henry needs water. As you work your way through the book, sequence the pictures from blacklines 65–66 in the pocket chart.

3. Ask the children to join in and sing the song once again, using the book, as a guide.

4. Help the children retell the whole song, using the pictures in the pocket chart as a reference. This is a fun song to dramatize. It can easily be pantomimed or you may wish to bring in props.

5. Divide the class into a Liza group and a Henry group and sing again. You may end up singing this hilarious song more times than you wish as it soon will be one of the children's favorites.

6. Tell the children that you know another song about a farmer. This farmer has a dog and the dog's name is Bingo. Teach the song to the children and sing several times, until the children have it memorized.

7. Using phonetic clues, develop the song, line by line, in the pocket chart. Sing again, reading from the pocket chart.

8. Now you are ready to add the hand claps in place of the missing letters. Sing once again, tracking as you go. When you come to the first letter in Bingo's name, turn the B card over so that the clapping hands are now visible. Tell the children that every time they see the hands clapping, they are to clap their hands one time instead of saying the letter. Thus, the song will now sound like this:

There was a farmer
Had a dog
And Bingo was his name-o
(clap) I N G O
(clap) I N G O
(clap) I N G O
And Bingo was his name-o.

66

9. Continue in this manner, turning over an additional letter and adding another clap (clap, clap, N G O) etc. until you have spelled the entire name.

10. It is fun to substitute the children's pets but we find that five letter names work the best. (There was a girl who had a cat and Sasha was her name-o, S A S H A etc.) Remember that you will need three sets of letters for each name.

There	was	a	farmer		
Had	a	dog			
And	Bingo	was	his	name-o	
(clap)	I	N	G	O	
(clap)	I	N	G	O	
(clap)	I	N	G	O	
And	Bingo	was	his	name-o.	

11. As an added treat and surprise to your class, you may wish to print the children's names which contain five letters and change the song to read:

There was a farmer
Had a friend
And Billy was his name-o etc.

12. You may wish to use this song during the various holidays of the year:

- There was a man who had a sack and Santa was his name-o...
- There was a rabbit had some eggs and Bunny...
- There was a leprechaun had some gold and O"Hara...
- There was a gobbler on the farm and Tommy...
- There was a witch who had a broom and Wanda...

 **Extension:** *Song Booklet*

1. Each child needs one piece of 12″ x 18″ light colored construction paper, one set of B I N G O letters and five hand clapping circles.
2. Fold the paper so it measures 9″ x 12″. (You may wish to have the paper pre-folded for younger children.)
3. Help the children print BINGO at the top of the folded construction paper. Using the draw with me technique, draw and color a picture of Bingo. For help in drawing, you may wish to refer to Beverly Armstrong's *Build a Doodle Farm.*
4. Cut the set of Bingo letters apart and then cut out the five handclapping circles. Color the letters and hands.
5. Open the construction paper so it measures 12″ x 18″. Across the middle, glue the five clapping hand circles, being careful not to place anything on the fold.
6. Lastly, to make the flap that covers the handclapping circle, the children carefully add glue to the top of the back side of the letter. Next, place the letter just above the circle and hold down until the glue dries. Now the letter may be lifted and creased so the clapping hands circle may be seen.

7. Sing the song, *Bingo*, with the children using their own folders. As the verses progress, the children lift the letter flaps and clap in place of the letters.

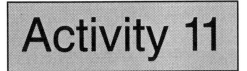

Activity 11

Wanda the Worm

Materials:

- Blacklines 69–77 for the *Wanda the Worm* big book
- Ten pieces of 12″ x 18″ construction paper, used for mounting the big book
- Blacklines 78–79 for the pocket chart
- Eight pieces of 5″ x 6″ tagboard cards to mount the above pictures
- Sentence strips
- Blacklines 80–81 for the extension booklet.
- Blackline 82 of the words for the extension booklet
- Blackline 83 of the cover for the extension booklet
- 9″ x 6″ white construction paper, five per child, for the booklet pages
- 9″ x 6″ green construction paper, two per child, for the front and back covers
- Laminating film or contact paper
- Loose leaf rings to bind the big book
- Small apples, one per child
- Samples of various types of apples
- Gummy worms, one per child

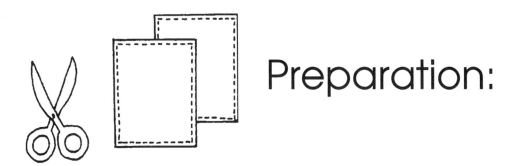

Preparation:

1. Duplicate blacklines 69–77 on white paper. Color and mount these pages on colored construction paper. Laminate or contact and bind with loose leaf rings.
2. Duplicate blacklines 78–79. Color, cut and mount on 5″ x 6″ tagboard cards. Contact or laminate.
3. Print the following on sentence strips Cut these into phrases to match the big book. Laminate or contact:

> **Wanda the worm crawled and crawled**
> **across the pasture**
> **around the pig pen**
> **over the garden hose**
> **past the scarecrow**
> **through the vegetable garden**
> **under the cornstalks**
> **and got back in time for her nap.**

4. Duplicate blackline 80 on red construction paper.
   Each child will need five apples.
5. Duplicate blackline 81 on green construction paper.
   Each child will need 6 worms.
6. Duplicate blackline 82 on white paper, one per child.
   Cut the sentences apart on the lines.
7. Duplicate blackline 83 on white paper, for the cover to the extension booklet, one per child.

8. Make a sample of the extension booklet the children will make, *Where's Wanda?*

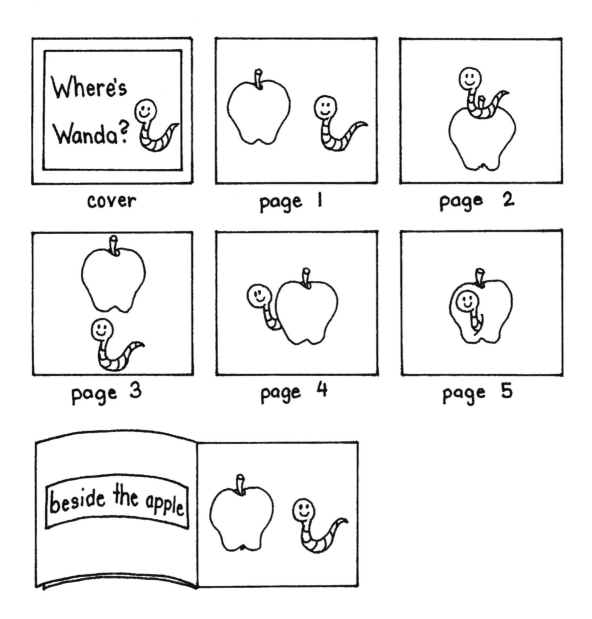

To make the cover, glue blackline 83 to a piece of colored 9″ x 6″ construction paper. Glue one worm opposite the title.

Prepare the remaining pages as shown in the illustration, using white construction paper. Please note the words are glued to the page opposite the picture. Add the back cover and staple.

9. On the day you will begin the extension booklet, use either an apple corer or the tip of a potato peeler to make a hole in each of the small apples. Inside each apple, insert a gummy worm, so that one end is left peeking out. Place these in a basket with some type of cover to hide the surprise! (You may wish to sprinkle a few drops of lemon juice in the holes to prevent the apples from turning brown.)

Procedure:

1. As an introduction to this activity, there are two books (which unfortunately are no longer in print) that we like to read. They are *The Big Fat Worm,* by Nancy Van Laan, and *Wiggly Worm,* by Jill Eggleton. If you cannot locate either of these we suggest you discuss with the children the fact that besides the animals, farms have other things that grow. List some of these on the chalkboard. (Apples, wheat, lettuce, carrots, corn, etc.)

2. Have available several types of apples and discuss what they look like – both on the outside and on the inside. Cut the apples and show the children the seeds and the core. Suggest to the children that sometimes you can find an additional surprise inside an apple...a worm!

3. Introduce the big book, *Wanda the Worm,* by telling the children you have a story about a worm that lives in an apple. Read and enjoy the story. Read again, using the my turn, your turn technique.

4. Develop the meaning of the language by helping the children dramatize each prepositional phrase. "Show me how you can crawl across something." (around, past, over etc.) This may be difficult for some five-year-olds as they are often confused by the terms *through* and *across.*

5. Using the pictures from blacklines 78–79, help the children sequence the story in the pocket chart.

6. Place the phrase strips somewhere in the room so they may be easily seen and obtained by the children.

7. Using phonetic clues, the children match each phrase to the appropriate pictures.

8. Read or chant the entire story from the pocket chart.

9. Take the pictures out of the pocket chart and distribute these to the class. The children then match the pictures to the appropriate phrases.

10. Now take the phrase strips and the pictures out of the pocket chart and distribute these to the class. The children rebuild the entire story using both the picture cards and the sentence strips. Check for accuracy by using the big book. Reread.

Extension: *Where's Wanda? Booklet*

1. Ask the children to tell you where Wanda lived (in an apple). Bring out the covered basket of wormy apples. Ask the class if they can guess what nutritious fruit that grows in an orchard on the farm might be in the basket. Distribute the apples, letting the children discover the worms! Stand back with a camera at the ready!

2. After the children have settled down, have them dramatize the following, using their apple and worm:

   • beside the apple
   • on top of the apple
   • under the apple
   • behind the apple
   • inside the apple

3. Introduce the story, *Where's Wanda?* using the sample you prepared previously. To make the booklet, each child needs two covers, the title for the front cover (blackline 83), five white construction paper pages, five apples, six worms and the phrases.

4. The children prepare the booklets as shown in the illustration under Preparation.

5. Read and enjoy the completed booklet. Don't forget to eat the apples and the worms!

Note: *The Color Box* theme has a delightful apple activity called The Little Red House. It is found on page 64, Activity 12.

Additional apple activities that are lots of fun to do are listed in the *Mathematics Their Way Newsletter XIII,* published by the Center For Innovation in Education. If this is not available to you, refer to pages 12.2–12.3 in the *Mathematics Their Way Summary Newsletter,* (Center for Innovation in Education, 19225 Vineyard Lane, Saratoga, California, 95070) and simply substitute an apple for the pumpkin.

Where's Wanda? is easily adapted to a Halloween theme. Change the title to *Where's The Ghost?* and substitute a ghost and pumpkin for the apple and worm. A nice surprise at the end is created by gluing two googly eyes in the center of the pumpkin to match the phrase, "inside the pumpkin." You may want to adapt this idea for other special events as well – *Where's the Easter Egg?, Where's Santa?* etc.

There Was An Old Lady Who Swallowed A Fly

Materials:

- *There Was An Old Lady Who Swallowed A Fly,* illustrated by Pam Adams
- *Sitting On The Farm* by Bob King
- *Spots Feathers and Curly Tails* by Nancy Tafuri
- Blacklines 84–85 of the Old Lady for the make-a-play
- Blacklines 86–87 for the pocket chart and for the make-a-play
- Seven pieces of tagboard cards to mount the above pocket chart pictures
- Blacklines 88–89 for the pocket chart
- Seven pieces of 5″ x 6″ tagboard cards to mount the above pocket chart pictures
- Pint-size sandwich baggie (with the expandable bottom), one per child (Do not get the baggies that have a white label area as it will show in the finished product.)
- For the extension, each child will need one piece of 12″ x 9″ (white) and one piece of 6″ x 9″ construction paper (any color)
- Sentence strips
- Laminating film or contact paper

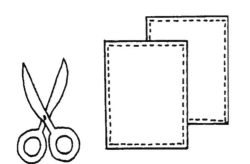

Preparation:

1. Duplicate blacklines 84–85 on heavy paper, one Old Lady per child.

Note: for your sample you will need to make a larger copy of the Old Lady – we suggest enlarging these two blacklines on tagboard or poster board and preparing it in the following manner:

Color and cut the two sections of the Old Lady, making sure to cut out the box in the apron and at the bottom of the top section, as noted. Matching the lines on the two pieces, glue the top section to the bottom section where indicated.

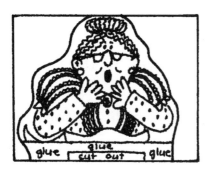 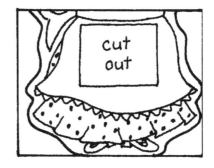

A ziploc baggie is stapled to the back and the Old Lady is now ready for action. Be sure to have the sandwich size baggie with the expandable bottom as the children will need the extra room when they put their hands in and out.

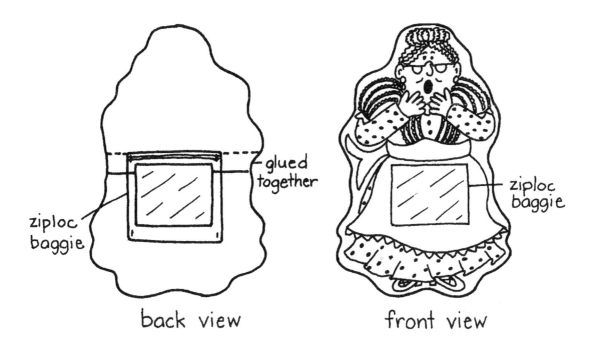

ziploc baggie

glued together

back view

ziploc baggie

front view

2. Duplicate blacklines 86–87, one of each per child and two of each for the teacher (one for your sample and one for the pocket chart). You may wish to enlarge a set of these for your sample.
3. Color, cut and mount one set of the above pictures on tagboard cards. Laminate or contact. These will be used for the pocket chart.
4. Color and cut a second set of pictures from blacklines 86–87, to be used in your sample. Glue these to a piece of tagboard or cardstock and cut around the bubbles. This is not necessary if you are able to duplicate directly on tagboard or cardstock. Laminate or contact.
5. On sentence strips, print the names of each of the animals found on blacklines 86–87. Cut into word cards and laminate or contact.
6. Duplicate blacklines 88–89. Color, cut and mount on 5″ x 6″ tagboard cards. Contact or laminate.

7. On eight sentence strips print the words found on the first page. You will be placing individual word cards directly on top of each animal name throughout the song. Thus, you will need to leave an additional bit of room after the printing of the words bug and the words frog. (Copyright prohibits us from giving you the words.) Contact or Laminate.

8. On individual word cards, print three copies of frog and five copies of each of the other animals. You will also need to print three copies of the word MUNCH! Contact or laminate.

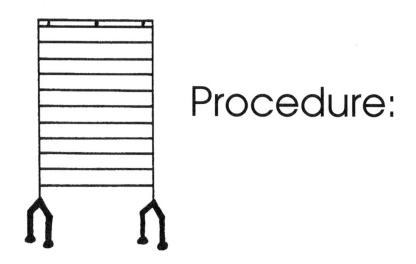

Procedure:

1. The song, *"The Old Lady Who Swallowed A Fly"*, is readily available on many children's recordings. We suggest you become familiar both with the tune, and with the sequence of each of the animals. For us, this book is a bit difficult to read from, and we know of no other published version at this time.

2. Use the book to introduce the song. Your children will soon join in on the repeated phrases. (Be sure to discuss the fact that this is a nonsense song and it could never ever happen. The pictures in the book will support this!)

3. Sing the song together again. Help the children sequence the animal pictures in the pocket chart. Ask the children if they notice anything as each new animal is added. (Each new animal is larger than the previous one.)

4. Sing again, using the animal pictures in the pocket chart as a guide. Using phonetic clues, help the children match the animal names to the appropriate pictures. Sing to check for accuracy.

5. Sing again, using your large sample. Let the children find the correct animal and drop it into her tummy. They will squeal with delight as they watch each new animal being added.

6. This is a good time to have the children brainstorm for a different sequence of animals (from smallest to largest) and list these on the chalkboard. It is fun to insert these new animals into the song and sing again.

7. Tell the children there is another story about some silly farm animals who cause problems for a little girl. This little girl tries to get a tiny bug off her knee and gets help from a series of increasingly larger animals. The publisher says this is a rollicking song but we have had great difficulty in understanding this. (No thumbs up.) We have had much better luck adapting the words to the tune *"Skip to my Lou"*. A word of caution–the word *"I"* needs to be emphasized in the fifth line in order to keep the meter.

8. Sing and enjoy the book, *Sitting On A Farm*. Discuss the pictures–especially the location of the telephone and the table in each new verse. Help the children trace the actions of the little squirrel and find out what makes him leave for good.

9. Sing again, sequencing the animal pictures in the pocket chart. Help the children compare and contrast the animals in both songs. Are there any that are the same?

10. In the pocket chart place the eight sentence strips, as well as the three MUNCH! cards. Sing and track the words. Have the children find the words that need to be replaced in the next verse. Continue singing the additional verses, placing the new animal names directly on top of the previous ones.

Extensions: *Old Lady Make-a-Play and Class Riddle Book*

Make-a-play – Each child needs one copy of blacklines 84–87. To make the Old Lady, follow the directions found under Preparation. For the animals, the children will only need to color and cut on the bubble line.

The children will enjoy singing the song again with their own copy of the Old Lady and the various animals. They can now take this song home to share with their families.

Class Riddle Book – Read and enjoy the book, *Spots Feathers and Curly Tails,* having the children predict the answers to the riddles. (You may need to discuss what a riddle is prior to reading this book.) Though this is a very simple book, it offers excellent rewrite opportunities. On the chalkboard, brainstorm for farm animals and their attributes.

| pig | chicken | cow | horse | duck | sheep |

- curly tail
- snout
- pink

- comb
- beak
- feathers
- wattle
- wings

- thin tail
- udder
- horns

- mane
- bushy tail

- webbed feet
- bill

- fluffy wool

81

Help each child choose one animal and one attribute for his or her page of the class book. Each child will need one piece of 9″ x 12″ colored construction paper and one piece of 6″ x 9″ construction paper in a contrasting color.

The children print the riddle at the top of the 9″ x 12″ construction paper. The lift-the-flap is cut from the 6″ x 9″ construction paper and attached to the page, carefully gluing only the top edge.
The children then illustrate and print the riddle's answer.

Bind together, add a cover, and read. This will be one of the most popular books in your class library.

Bibliography

Although we have made every effort to locate the current copyright holders of the materials used in this theme book, some we were unable to trace. We will be happy to correct any errors or omissions.

Adams, Pam, *There Was An Old Lady Who Swallowed A Fly*, Child's Play, England, 1973.

Armstrong, Beverly, *Build A Doodle Farm–A Step-By-Step Line Drawings To Improve Visual Perception*, The Learning Works, Inc., Santa Barbara, CA, 1985.

Aruego, Jose and Dewey, Ariane (illustrators), *Five Little Ducks*, Crown Publishers, Inc., New York, 1989.

Brown, Ruth, *The Big Sneeze*, Lothrop, Lee & Shepard Books, New York, 1985.

Brown, Margaret Wise, *Big Red Barn*, Scholastic Inc., New York, 1990.

Bruna, Dick, *Farmer John*, Price/Stern/Sloan, Los Angeles, 1984.

Carrick, Donald, *Milk*, Greenwillow Books, New York, 1985.

Catz, Bobbi and Moseley, Keith, *The Fox in the Farmyard*, Intervisual Communications, Inc., Mexico, 1985.

Cook, Brenda, *All About Farm Animals*, Doubleday, New York, 1988.

Cowley, Joy, *The Farm Concert*, Shortland Publications Limited, New Zealand, 1983. (distributed by The Wright Group)

Cowley, Joy and Melser, June, *Mrs. Wishy Washy*, Shortland Publications Limited, New Zealand, 1980. (distributed by The Wright Group)

Cowley, Joy and Melser, June, *One Cold Wet Night*, Shortland Publications Ltd., New Zealand, 1984. (distributed by The Wright Group)

de Paola, Tomie, *Charlie Needs A Cloak*, Prentice-Hall, Inc., New Jersey, 1973.

Dunn, Judy, *The Little Rabbit*, Random House, New York, 1980.

Eggleton, Jill, *Wiggly Worm*, Shortland Publications, Limited, Distributed by The Wright Group, 1986. (not available at this time from Wright Group.)

Emberly, Ed, *Ed Emberly's Drawing Book of Animals*, Little, Brown and Company, Boston, 1970.

English, Tracey, *Old MacDonald Had a Farm–A Lift & Look Counting Book, An Artists & Writers Guild Book*, Golden Books, Western Publishing Company, Inc., New York, 1993.

Eye Openers–*Farm Animals*, Aladdin Books, Macmillan Publishing Company, 1991.

Galdone, Paul, *Cat Goes Fiddle-i-fee*, Clarion Books, Ticknor & Fields: A Houghton Mifflin Company, New York, 1985.

Gammell, Stephen, *Once Upon MacDonald's Farm...*, Four Winds Press, New York, 1981.

Geisert, Arthur, *PIGS from A to Z*, Houghton Mifflin, Boston, 1986.

Gibbons, Gail, Farming, *Holiday House*, New York, 1988.

Gibbons, Gail, *The Milk Makers*, Macmillan, New York, 1985.

Ginsburg, Mirra, *The Strongest One of All*, Greenwillow Books, New York, 1977.

Hall, Donald, *Ox-Cart Man*, The Viking Press, New York, 1979.

Hayes, Sarah, *Nine Ducks Nine*, Lothrop, Lee & Shepard Books, New York, 1990.

Hellen, Nancy, *Old MacDonald Had a Farm*, Orchard Books, New York, 1990.

Hill, Eric, *Spot Goes to the Farm*, G.P. Putnam's Sons, New York, 1987.

Isenbart, Hans-Heinrich, *Baby Animals On The Farm*, G.P. Putnam's Sons, New York, 1981.

Jacobs, Leland, Goodnight *Mr. Beetle*, DLM Teaching Resources, Allen, Texas, 1987.

Kamen, Gloria, *"Paddle," said the Swan*, Atheneum, New York, 1989.

King, Bob, *Sitting On The Farm*, Orchard Books, New York, 1991.

Lindbergh, Reeve, *The Midnight Farm*, Dial Books for Young Readers, New York, 1987.

Luton, Mildred, *Little Chick's Mothers and All The Others*, Puffin Books, New Jersey, 1985.

McGovern, Ann, *Too Much Noise,* Houghton Mifflin Company, Boston, 1967.

McMillan, Bruce (photo-illustrator), *Mary Had A Little Lamb,* Scholastic Hardcover, New York, 1990.

Moncure, Jane Belk, *Away Went the Farmer's Hat,* Childrens Press, Chicago, 1988.

Most, Bernard, *The Cow That Went Oink,* Harcourt Brace Jovanovich, Publishers, New York, 1990.

Miller, Jane, *Farm Noises,* Simon & Schuster Books for Young Readers, New York, 1989.

Miller, Jane, *Farm Alphabet Book,* Prentice-Hall, Inc., New Jersey, 1983.

Miller, Jane, *Farm Counting Book,* Simon & Schuster, New York, 1983.

Munsch, Robert, *Pigs,* Annick Press Ltd., Toronto, Canada, 1989.

Nichol, bp, *Once A Lullaby,* Greenwillow Books, New York, 1986.

Nodset, Joan L., *Who Took The Farmer's Hat?,* Scholastic Inc., New York, 1963.

Pearson, Tracey Campbell, *Old MacDonald Had a Farm,* Dial Books for Young Readers, (A Pied Piper Book–paperback), New York, 1986.

Pomerantz, Charlotte, *One Duck, Another Duck,* Greenwillow Books, New York, 1984.

Provensen, Alice and Martin, *Our Animal Friends At Maple Hill Farm,* A Random House Book, New York, 1974.

Provensen, Alice and Martin, *The Year At Maple Hill Farm,* Aladdin Books, New York, 1988.

Pryor, Bonnie, *Greenbrook Farm,* Simon & Schuster, New York, 1991.

Rae, Mary Maki (illustrator), *The Farmer In The Dell,* Puffin Books, New York, 1990.

Roffey, Maureen, *Home Sweet Home,* W. S. Cowell Ltd., Ipswich, 1982.

Rylant, Cynthia, *Night In The Country,* Bradbury Press, New York, 1986.

Schenk de Regniers, Beatrice, *Going for a Walk,* Harper & Row, New York, 1961.

See How They Grow Series, Dorling Kindersley, Inc., New York, 1992. (Foal, Duck, Calf, Chick, Lamb, Rabbit)

Shaw, Nancy, *Sheep in a Jeep,* Houghton Mifflin, Boston, 1986.

Spanjian, Beth, *Baby Lamb,* Longmeadow Press, Connecticut, 1988.

Tafuri, Nancy, *Early Morning In The Barn,* Picture Puffin Books, New York, 1986.

Tafuri, Nancy, *Spots Feathers and Curly Tails,* Greenwillow Books, New York, 1988.

Van Laan, Nancy, *The Big Fat Worm,* Alfred A. Knopf, New York, 1987.

Waddell, Martin, *Farmer Duck,* Candlewick Press, Cambridge, Mass., 1992.

Westcott, Nadine Bernard (illustrator), *There's a Hole in the Bucket,* HarperTrophy, Mexico, 1993.

Wildsmith, Brian, *Toot, Toot,* Oxford University Press, New York, 1985.

Williams, Sue, *I Went Walking,* Harcourt Brace Jovanovich, Publishers, New York, 1989.

Blacklines

E IE IO

Cut
out

1

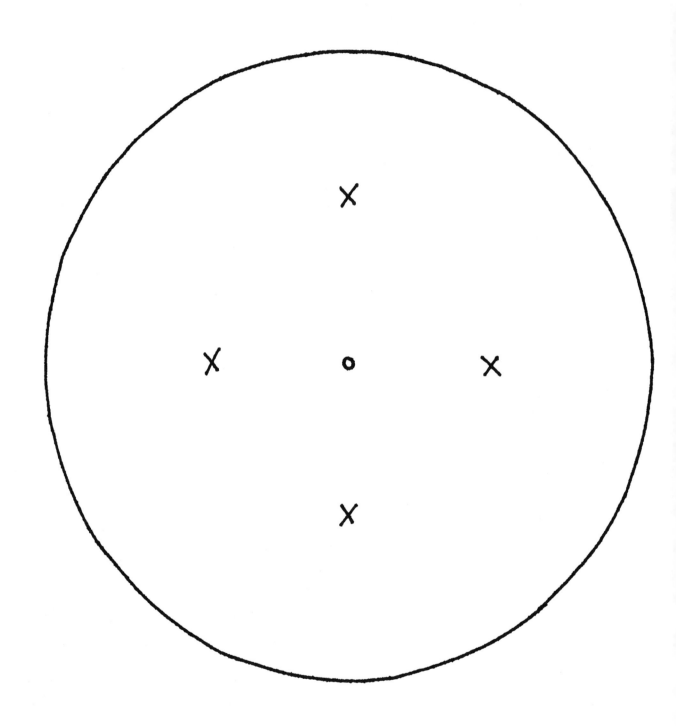

4

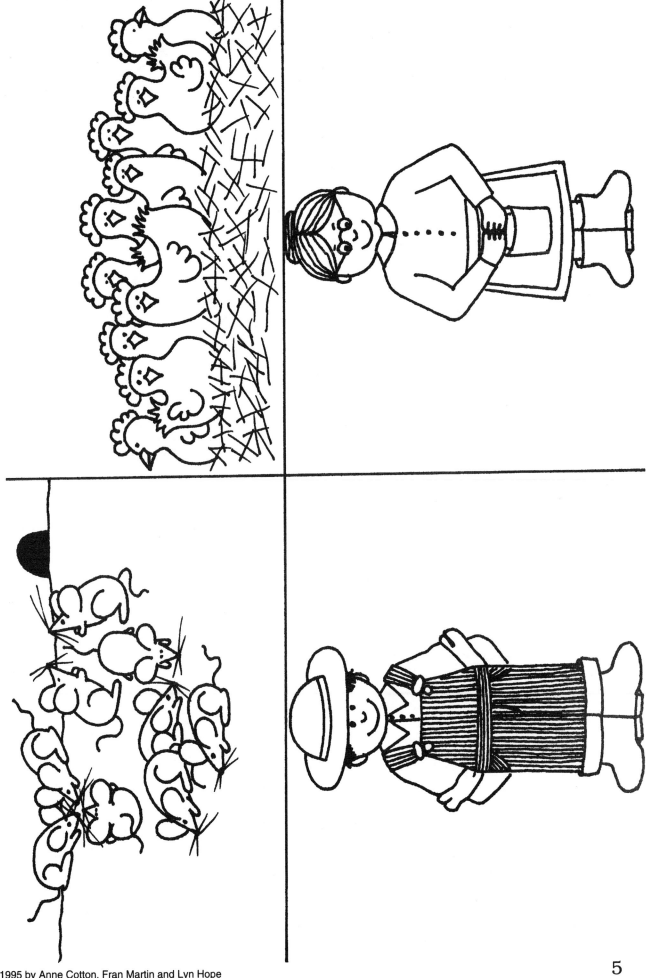

5

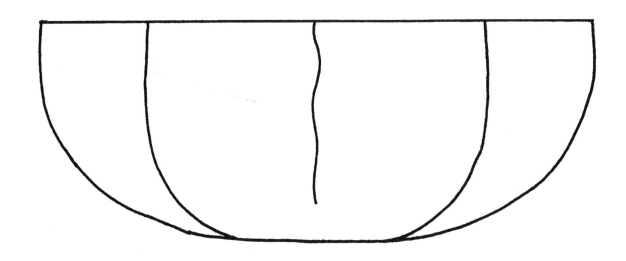

6

8

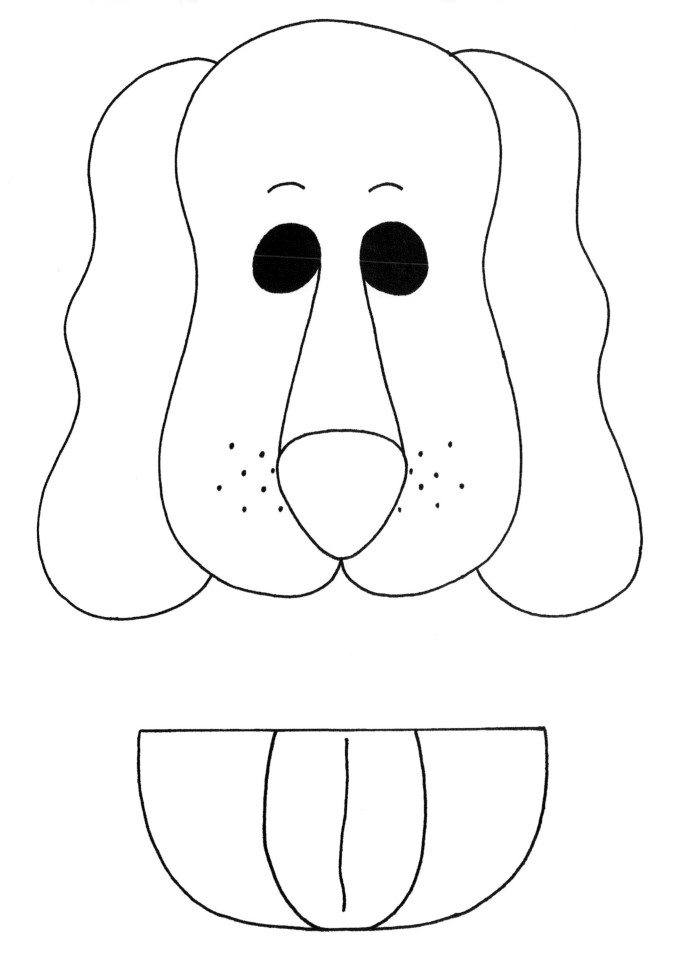

10

11

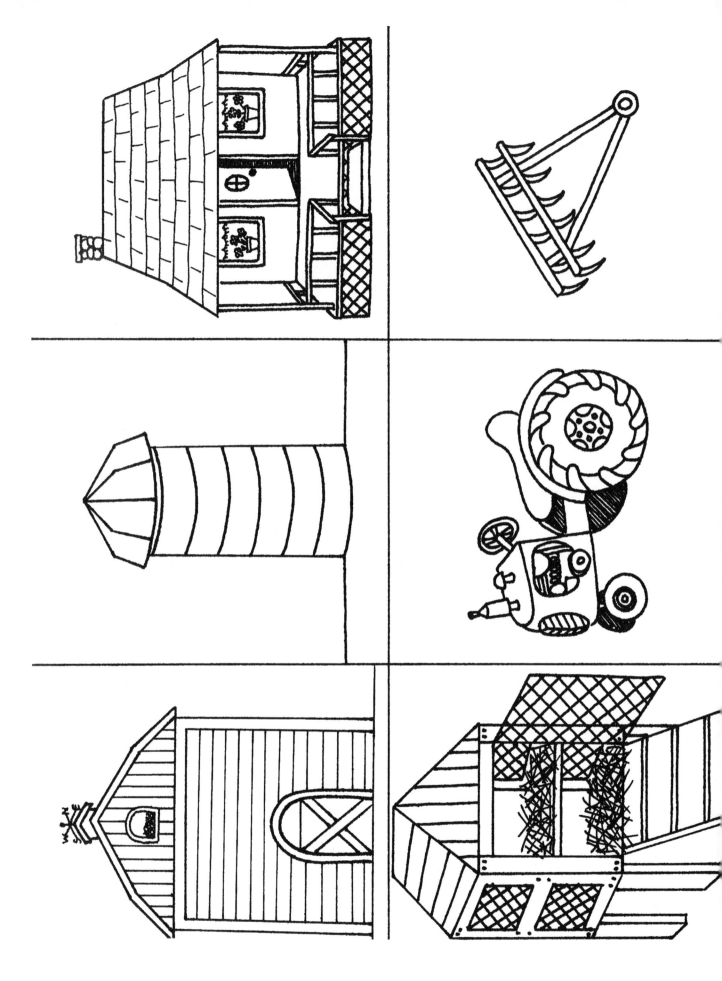

12

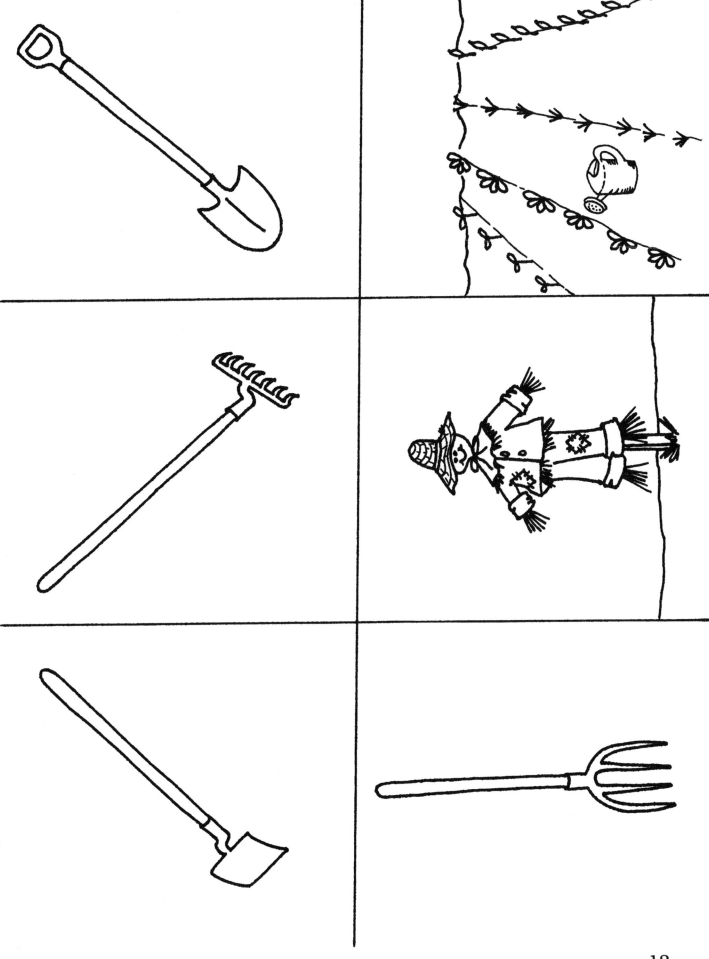

14

15

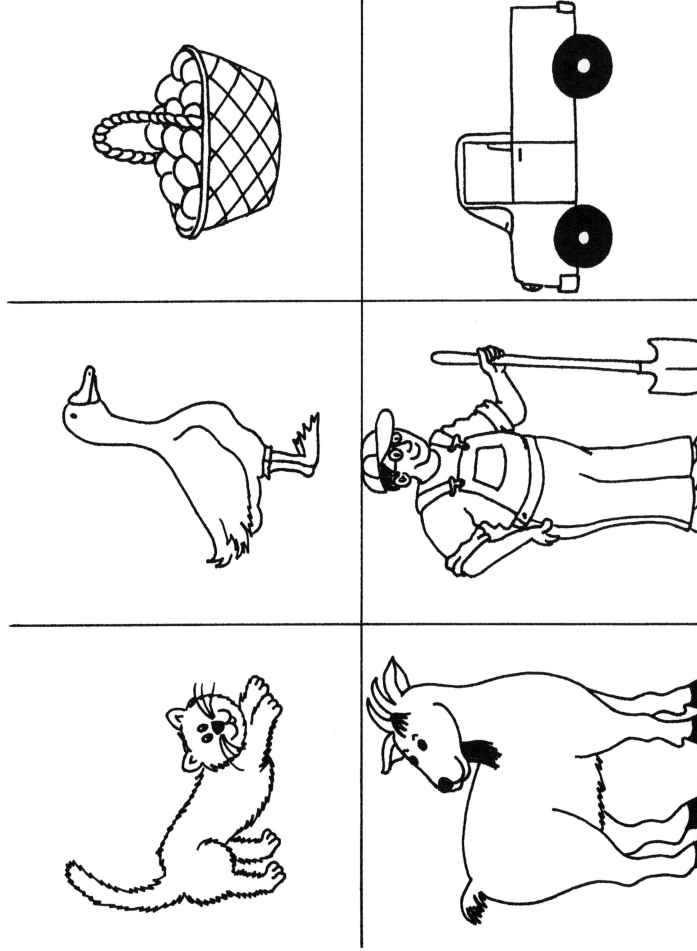

_____ _____ had a _____, EIEIO
And in this _____ _____ had a _____,
EIEIO
With a _____ _____ here and a _____
_____ there,
Here a _____, there a _____,
Everywhere a _____ _____
_____ _____ had a _____, EIEIO.

19

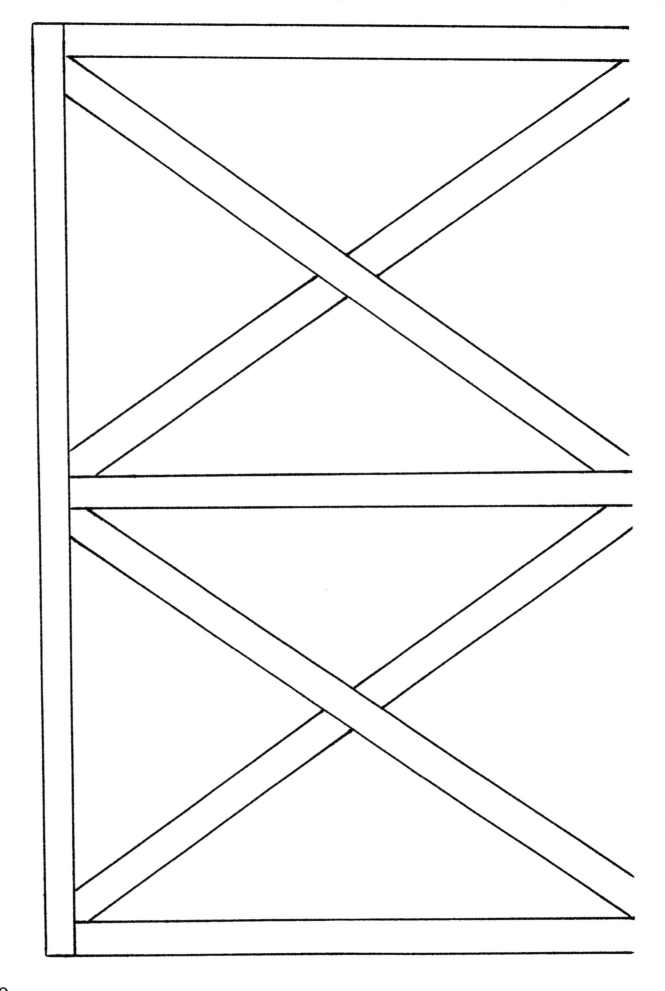

20

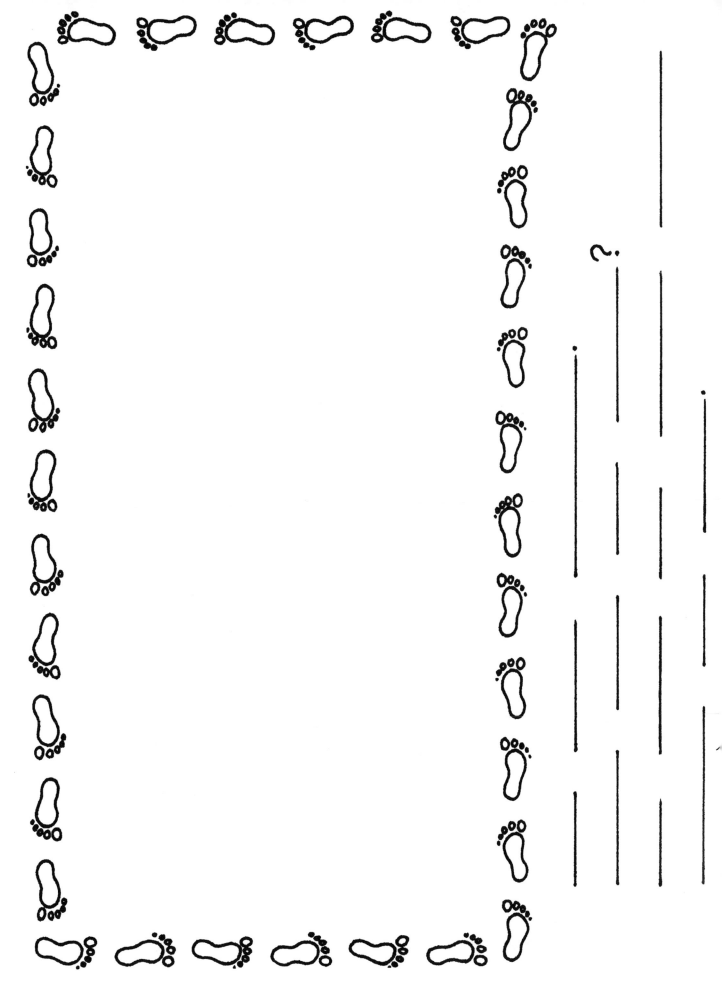

farmer	wife	child
nurse	dog	cheese
cat	rat	

- -

farmer	wife	child
nurse	dog	cheese
cat	rat	

26

27

28

29

30

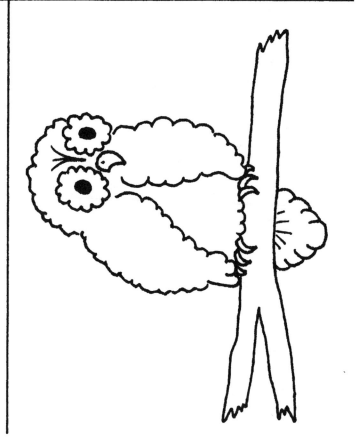

31

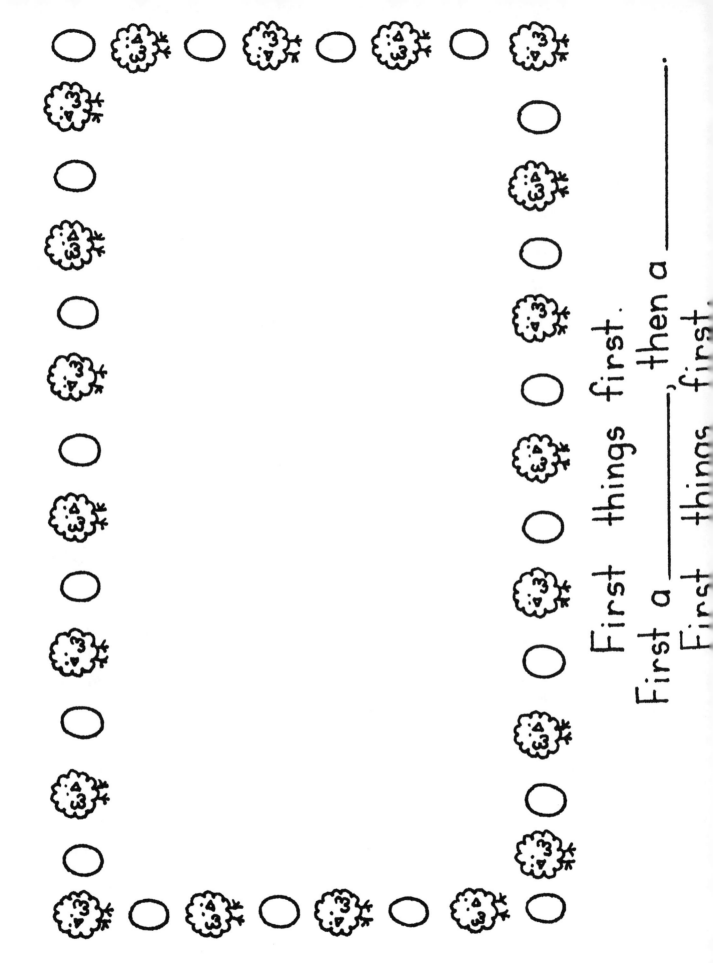

First things first.

First a _____, then a _____.

First things first.

33

ONE DUCK, ANOTHER DUCK

34

36

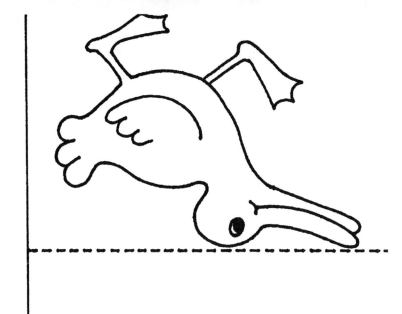

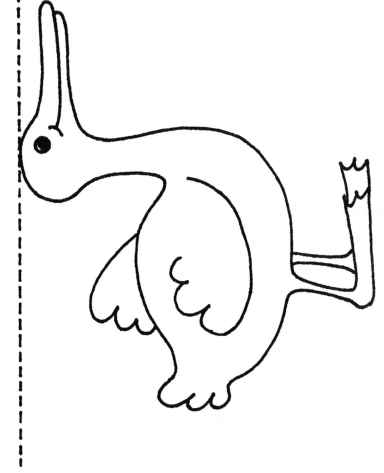

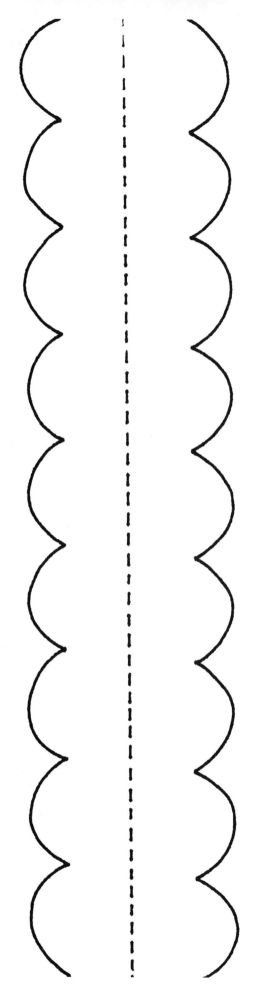

38

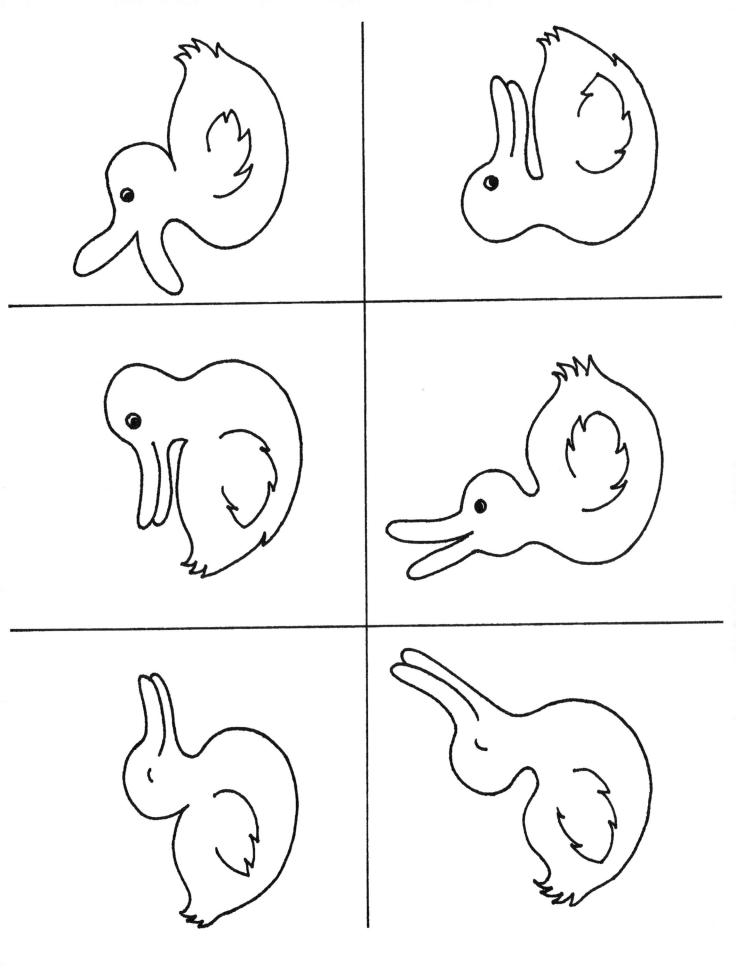

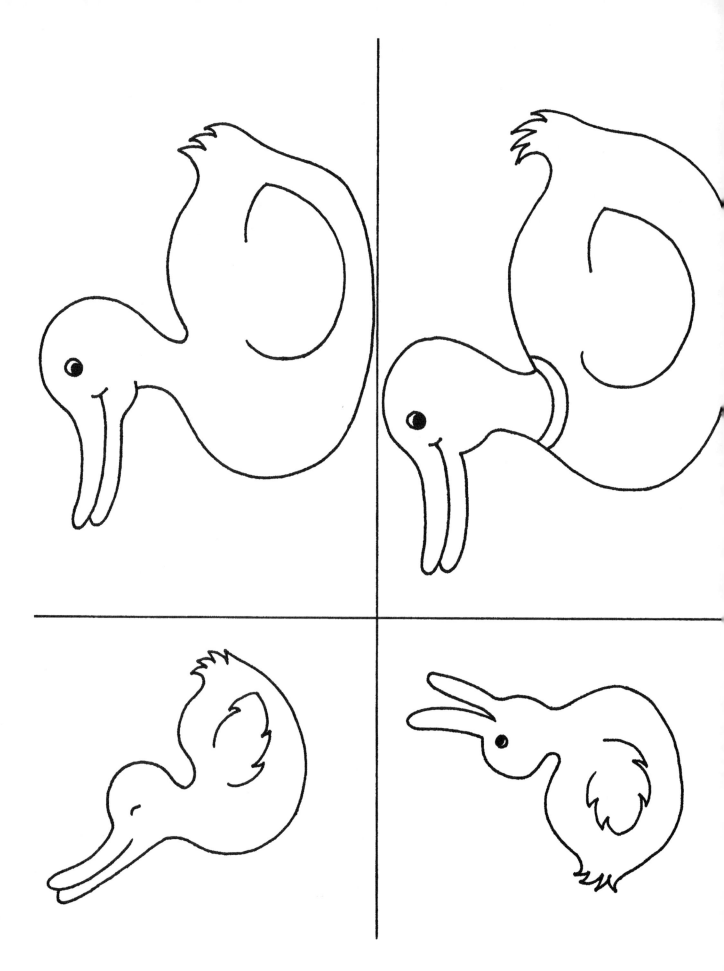

40

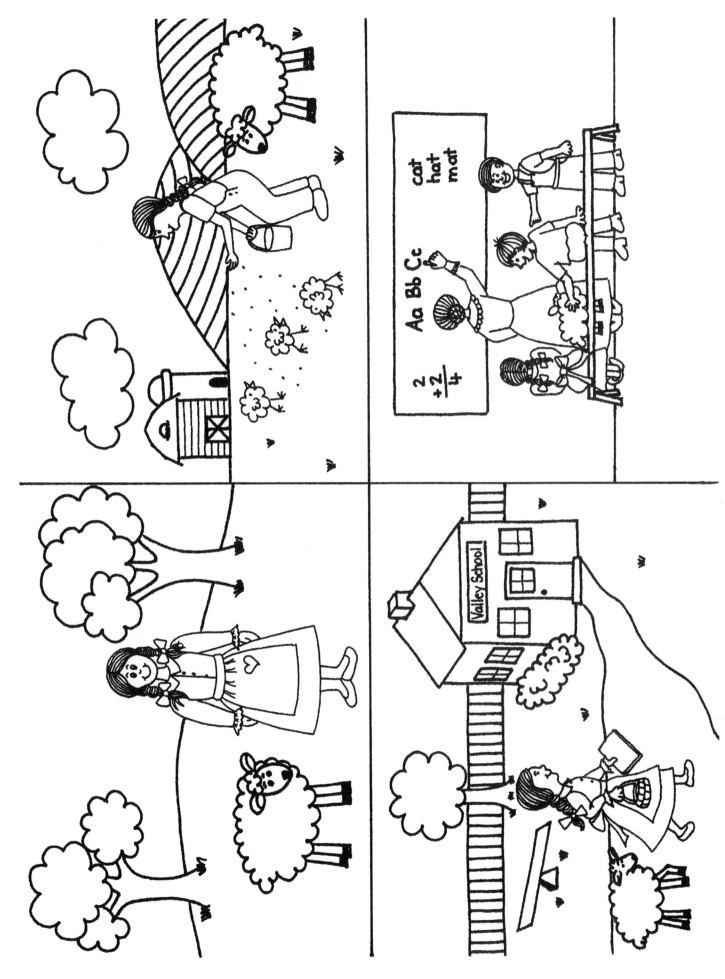

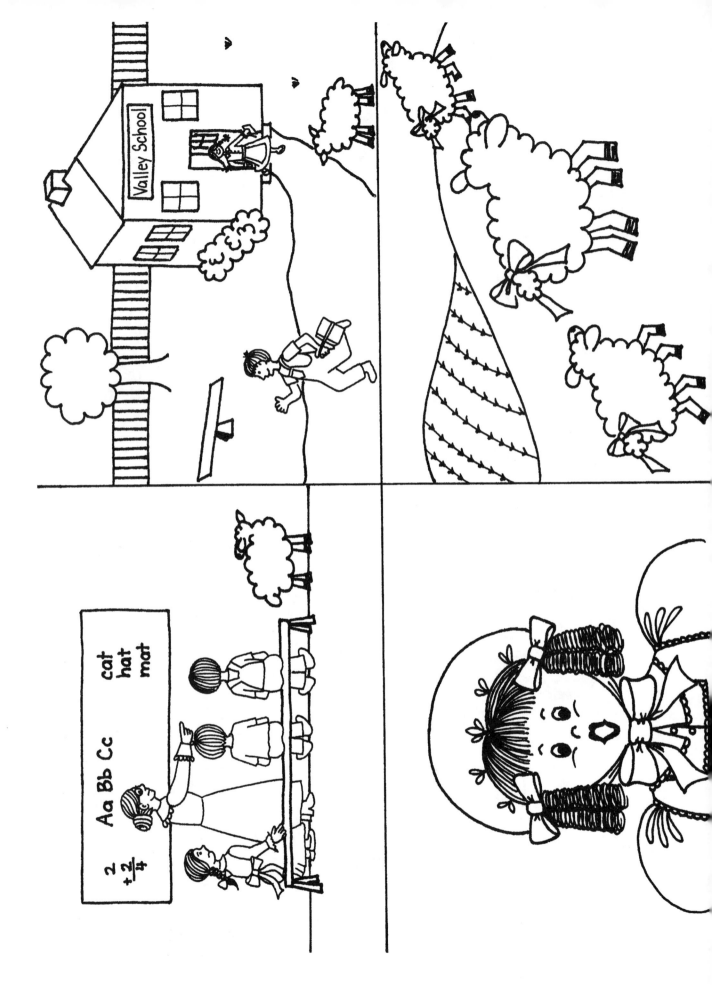

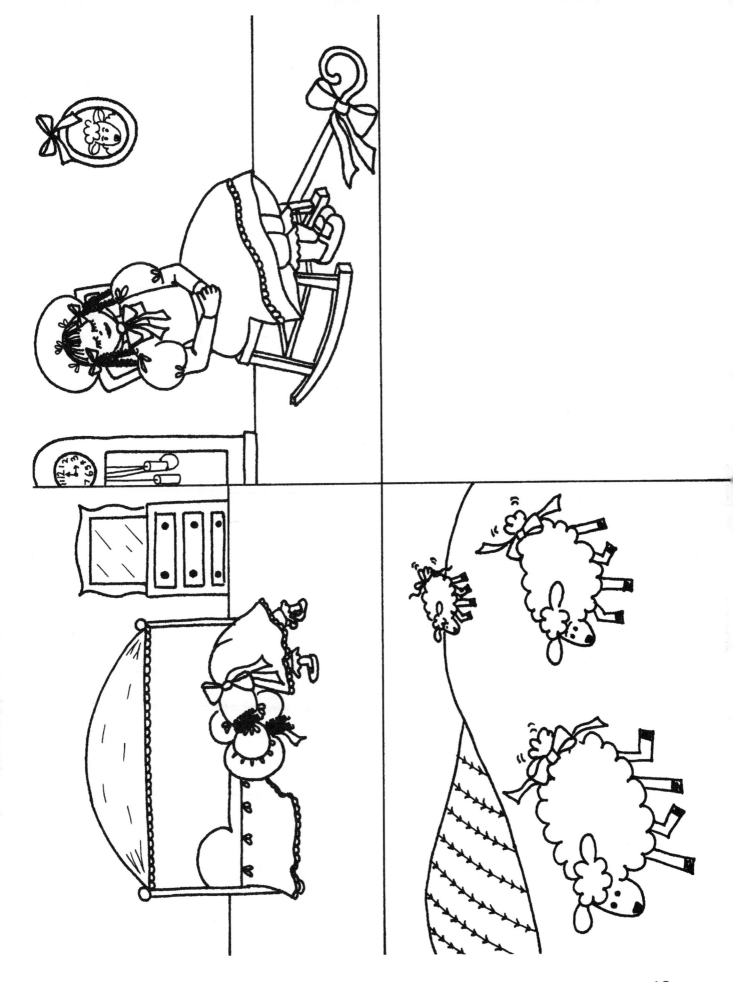

43

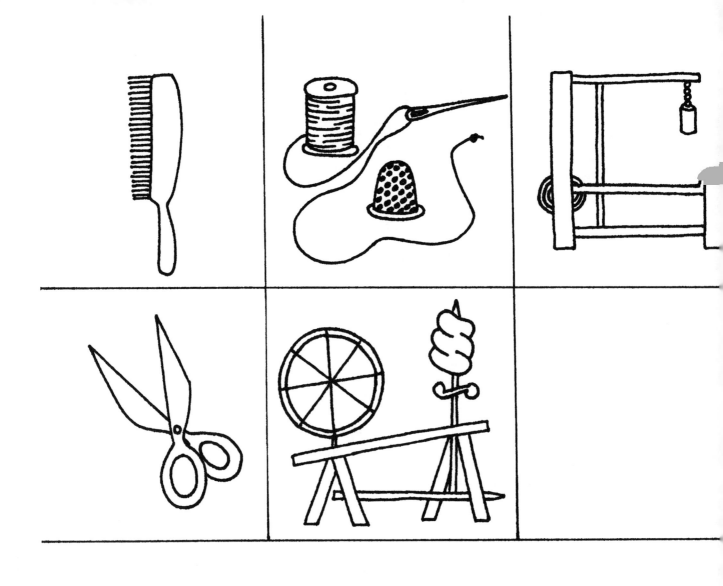

spin	sew	shear
card	weave	
1	2	3	4	5

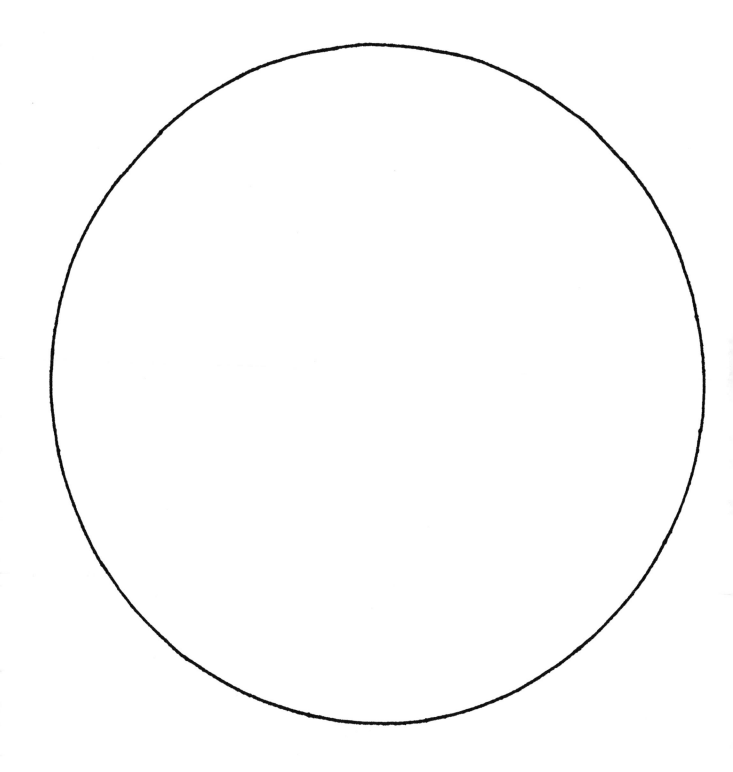

45

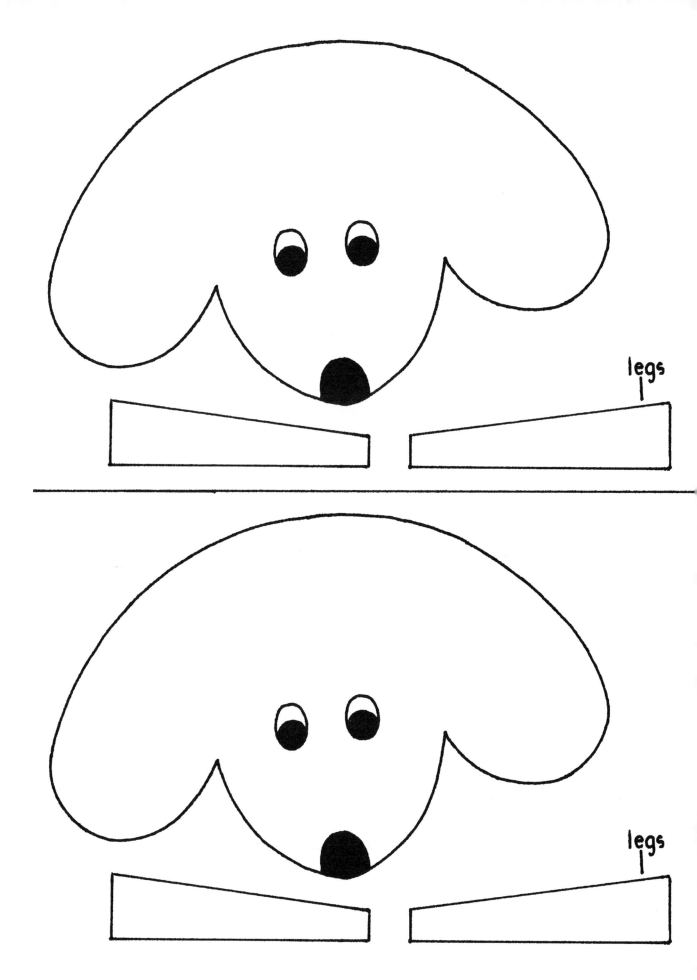

legs

legs

46

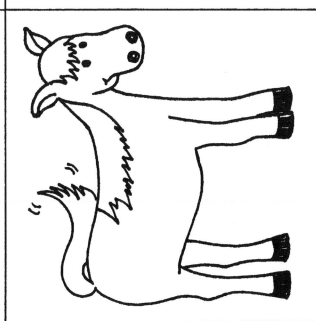

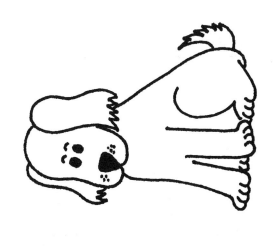

47

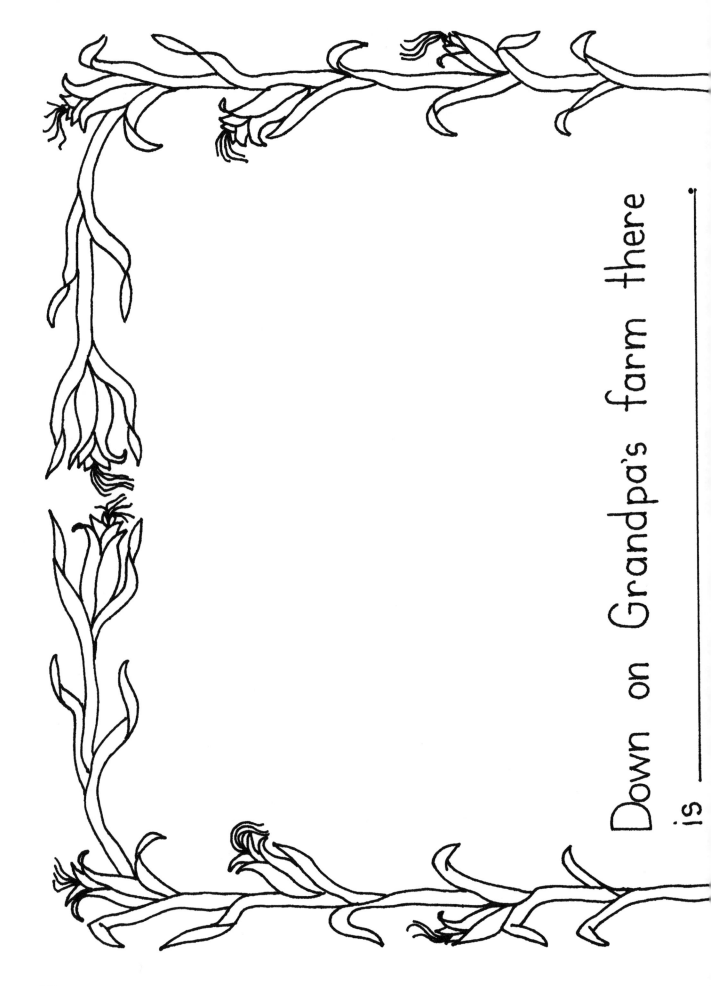

Down on Grandpa's farm there

is _____.

48

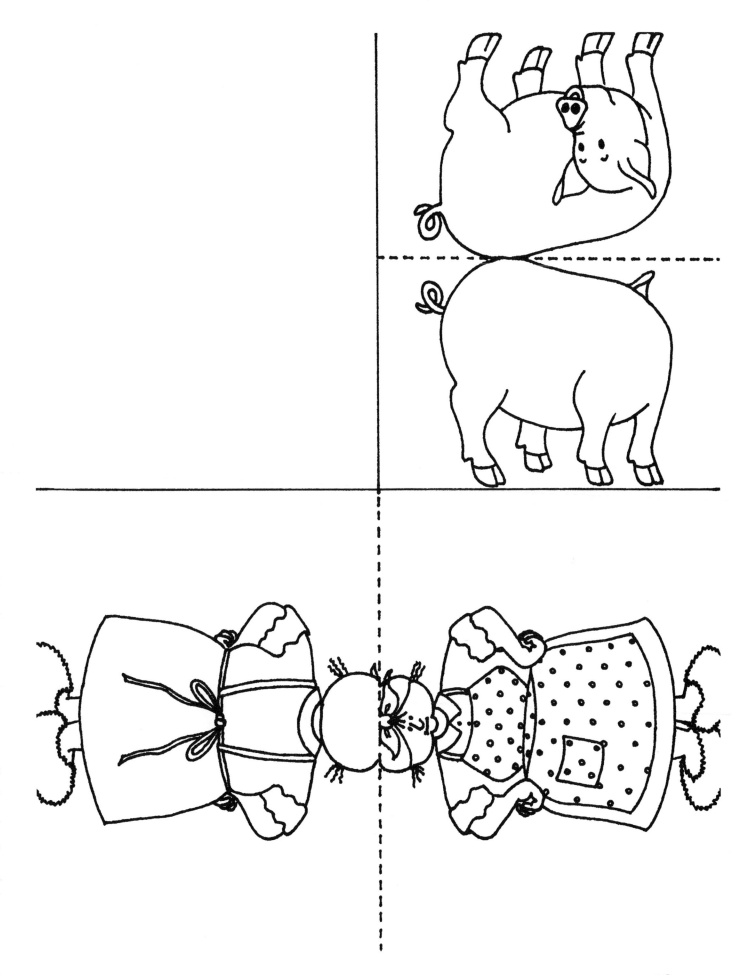

49

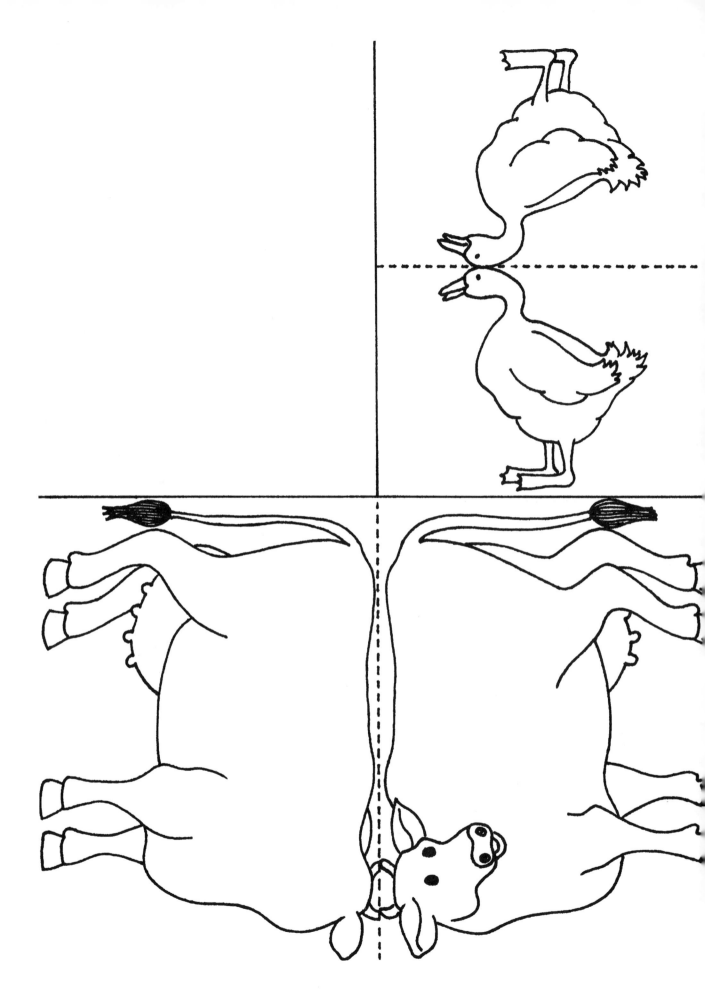

50

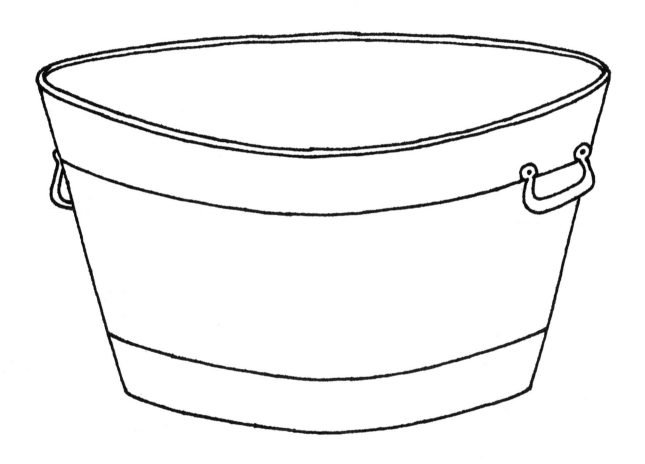

52

54

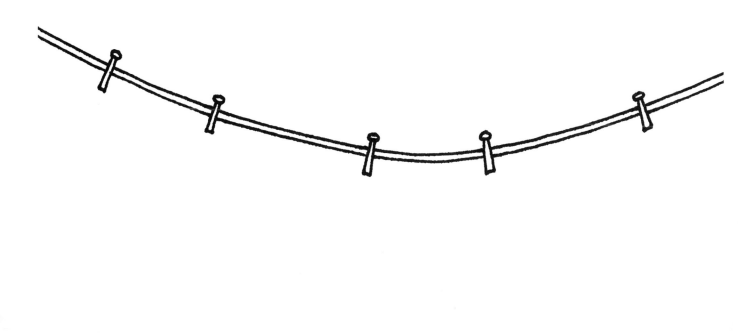

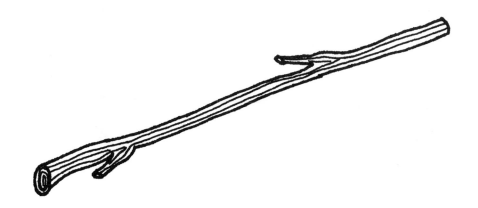

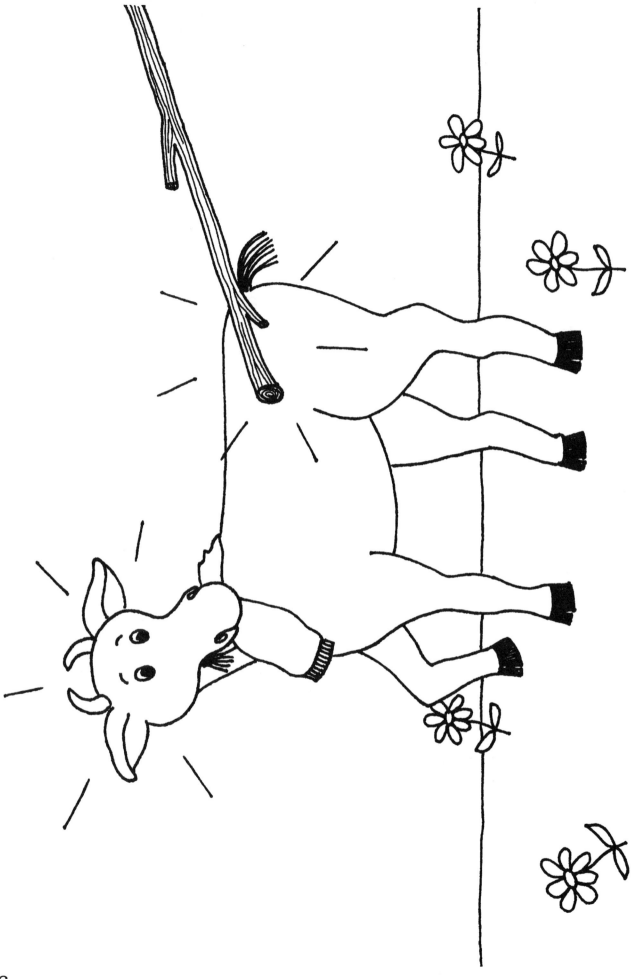

56

57

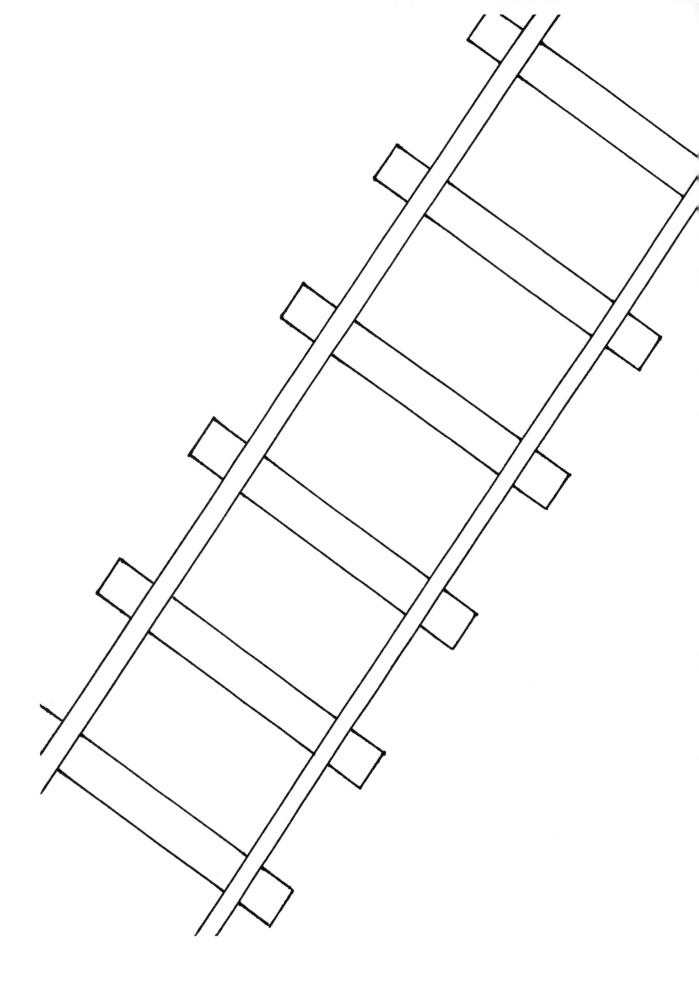

58

60

61

Here lies
Bill Grogan's
Goat
Met a train!
June 5, 1900

62

64

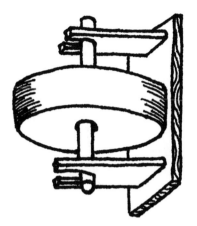

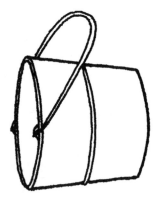

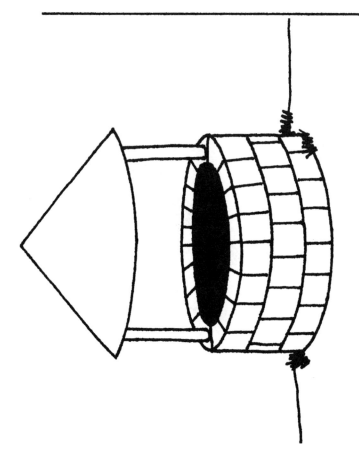

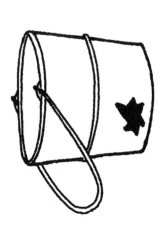

66

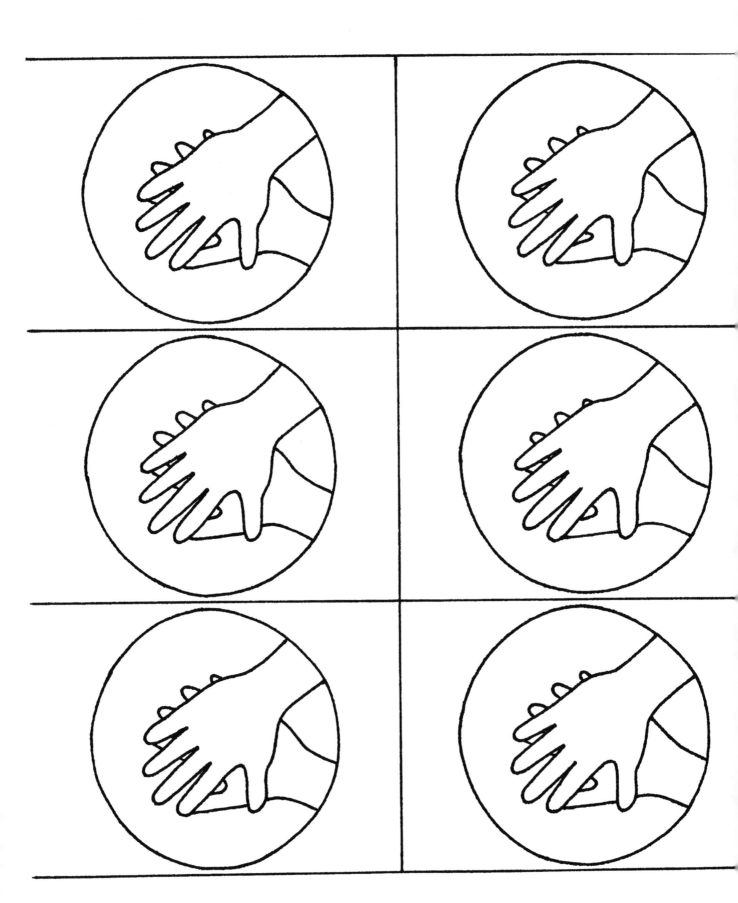

68

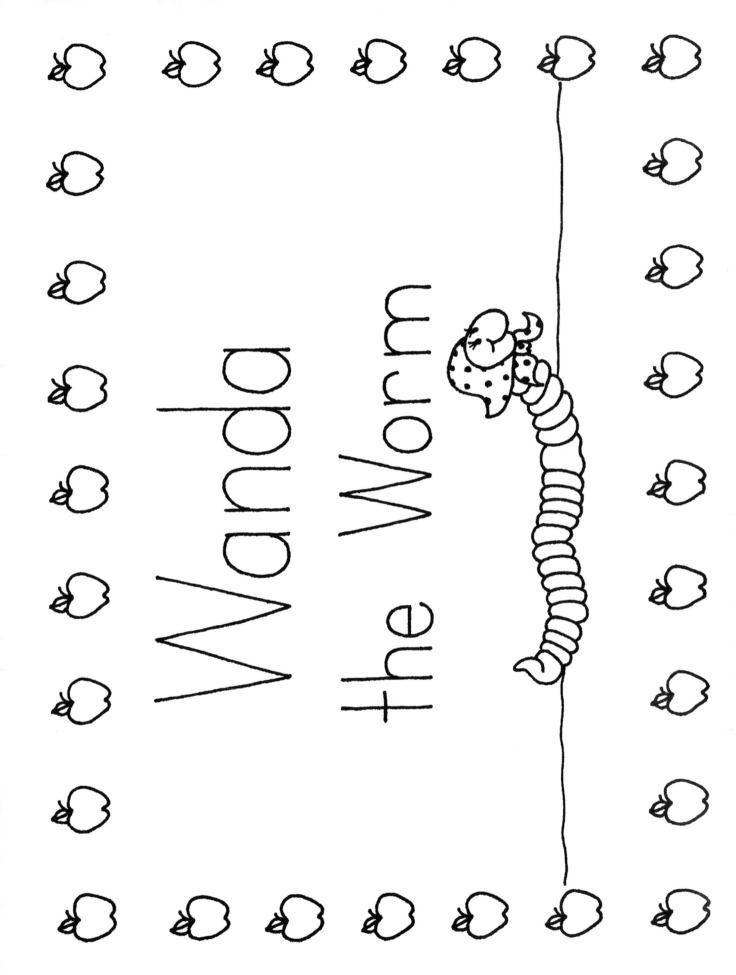

Wanda
the Worm

Wanda the worm crawled and crawled

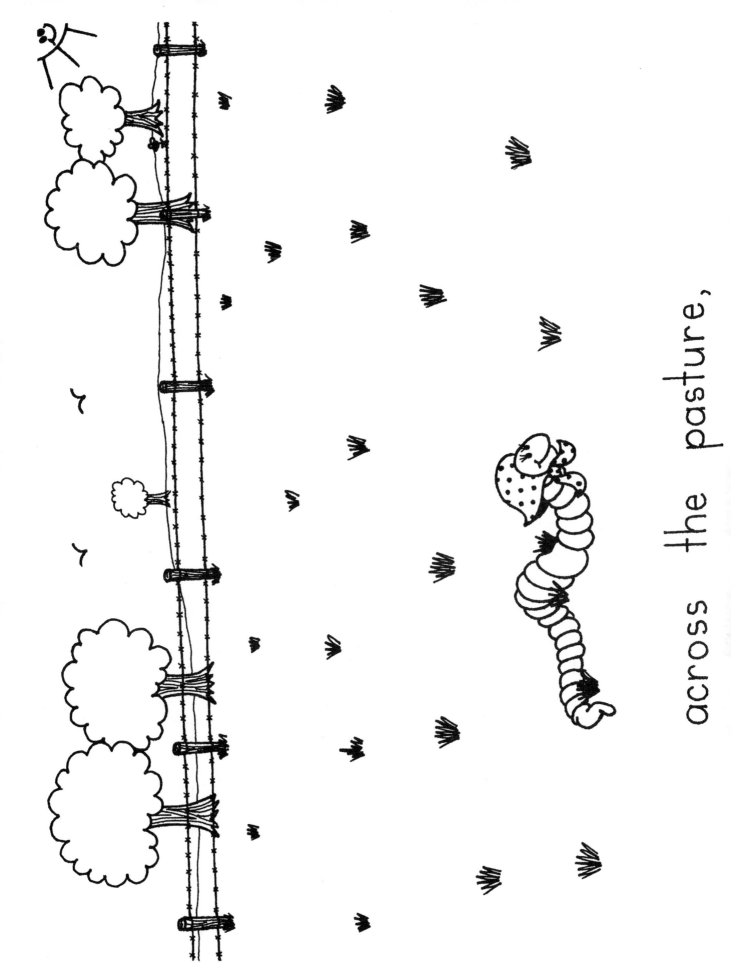

across the pasture,

around the pig pen,

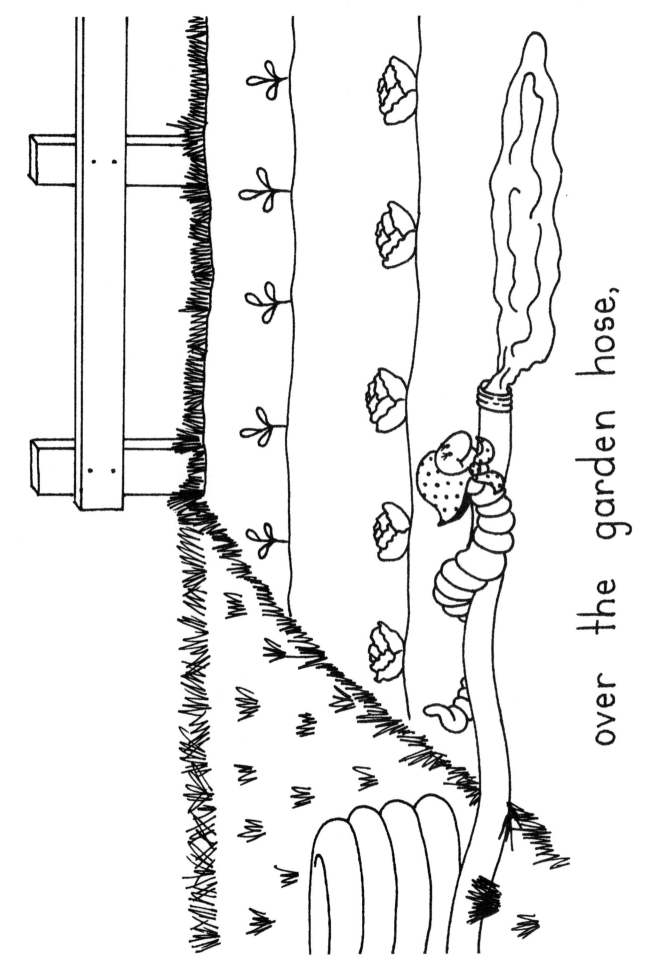

over the garden hose,

73

past the scarecrow,

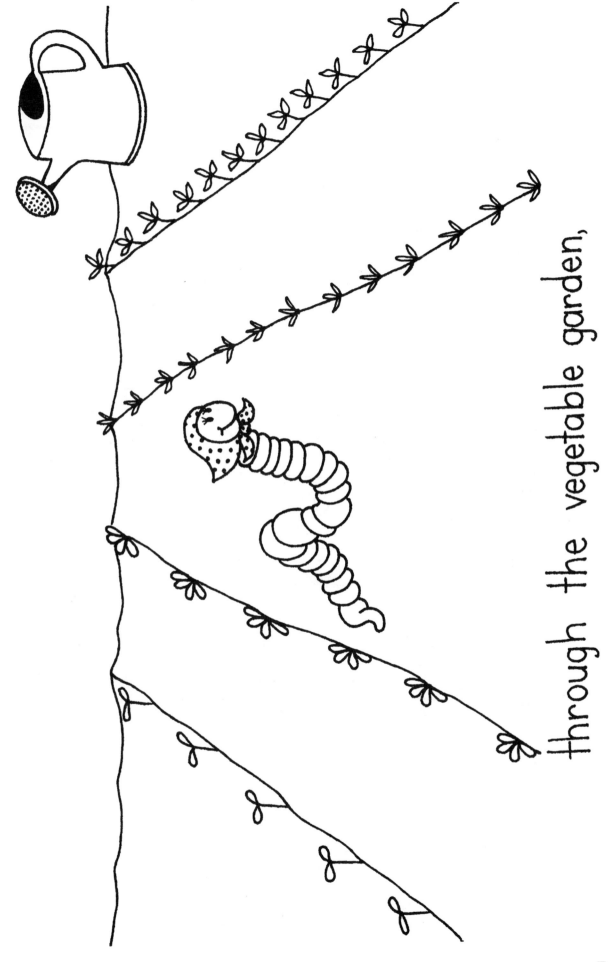

through the vegetable garden,

75

under the cornstalks,

76

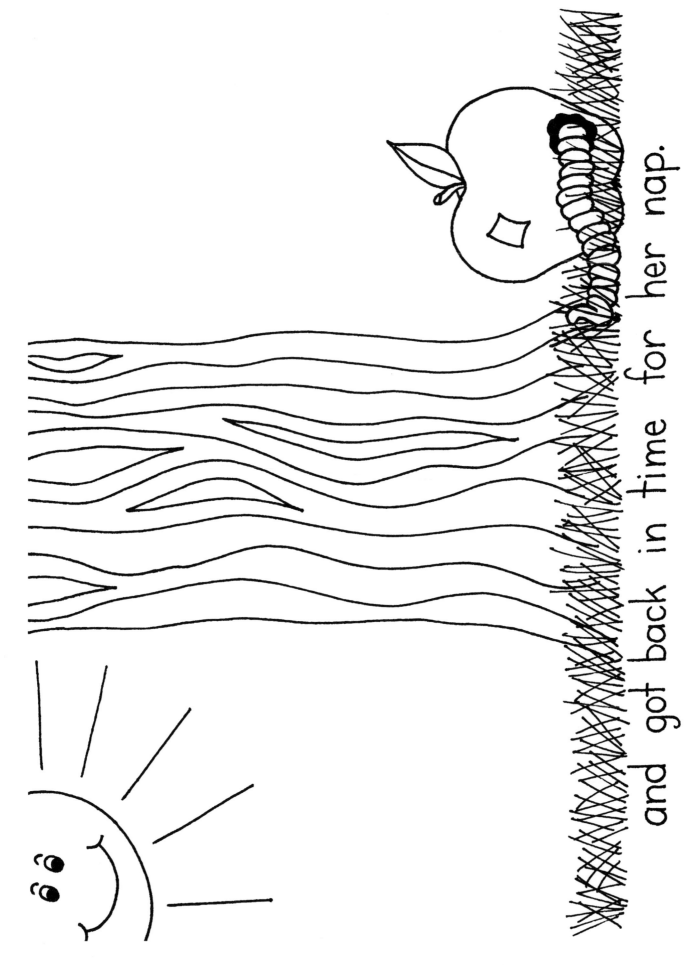

and got back in time for her nap.

77

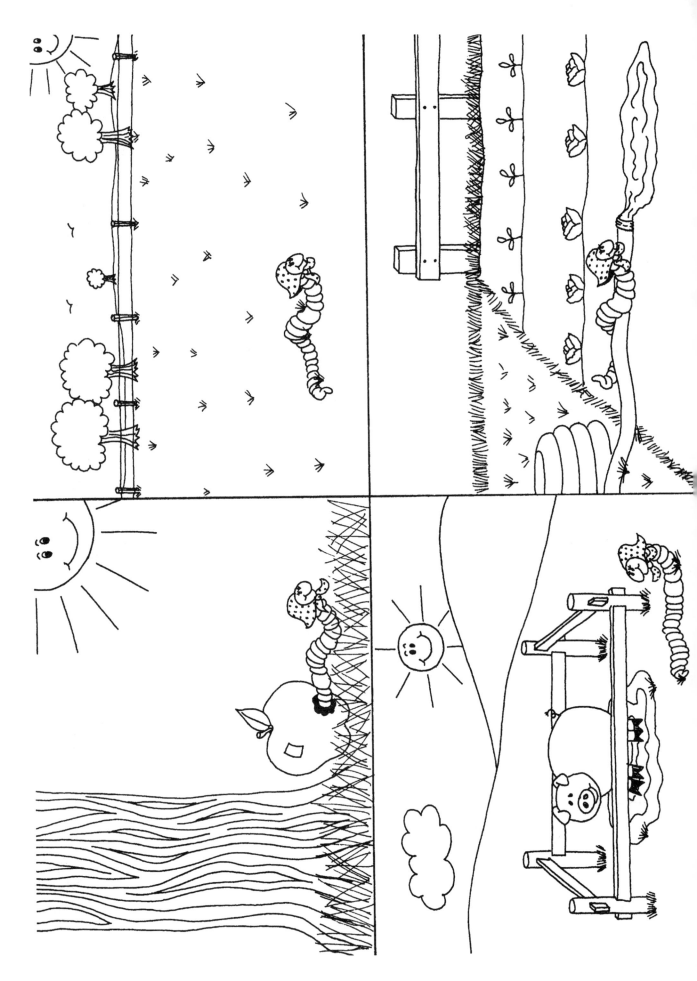

78

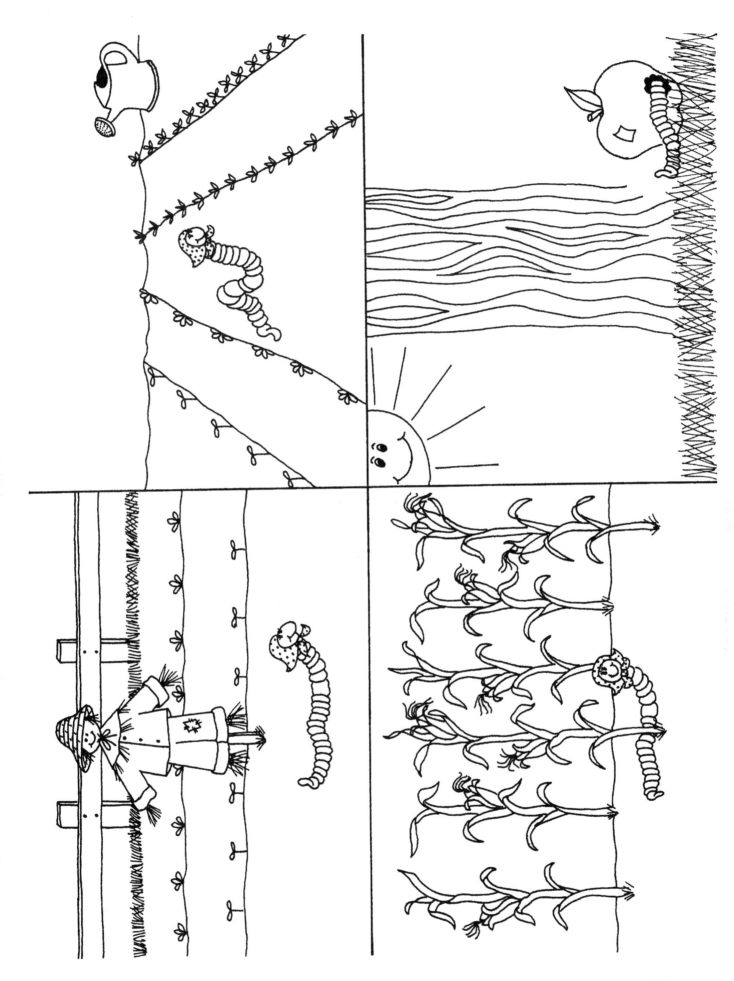

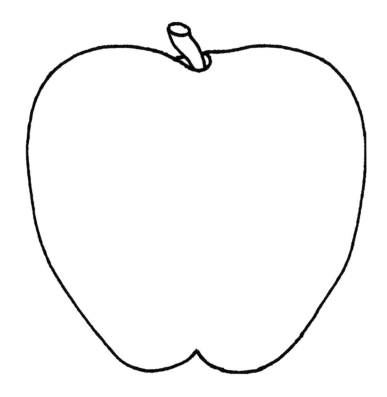

80

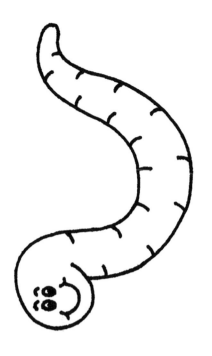 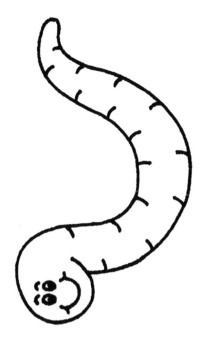

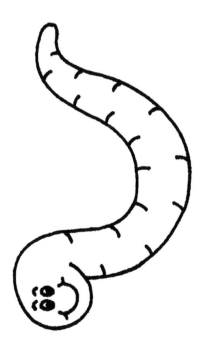 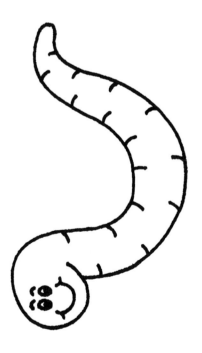

81

beside the apple
on top of the apple
under the apple
behind the apple
inside the apple

Where's Wanda?

Where's Wanda?

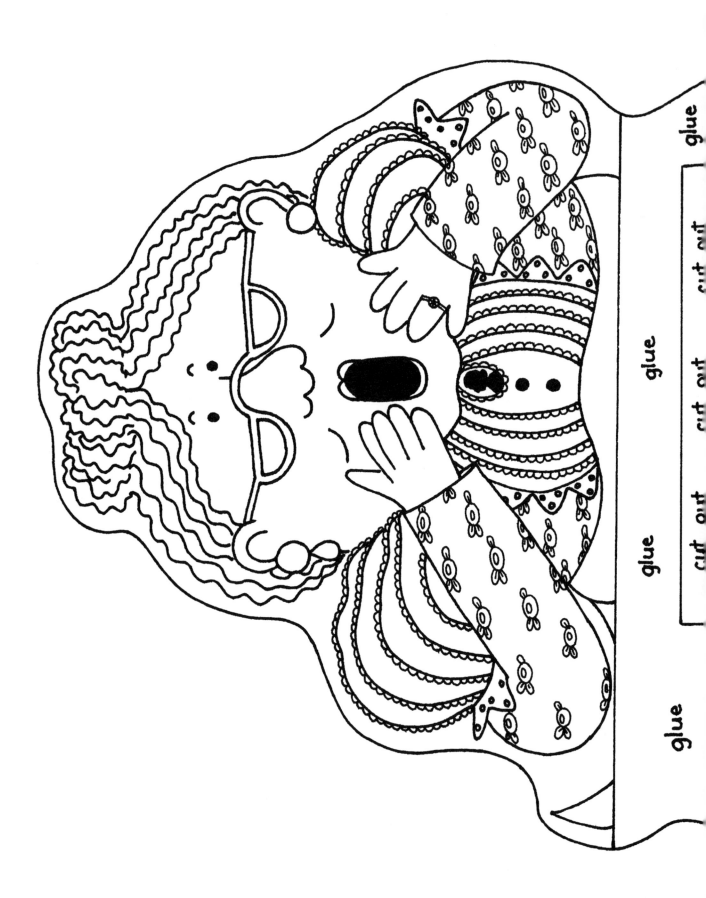

84

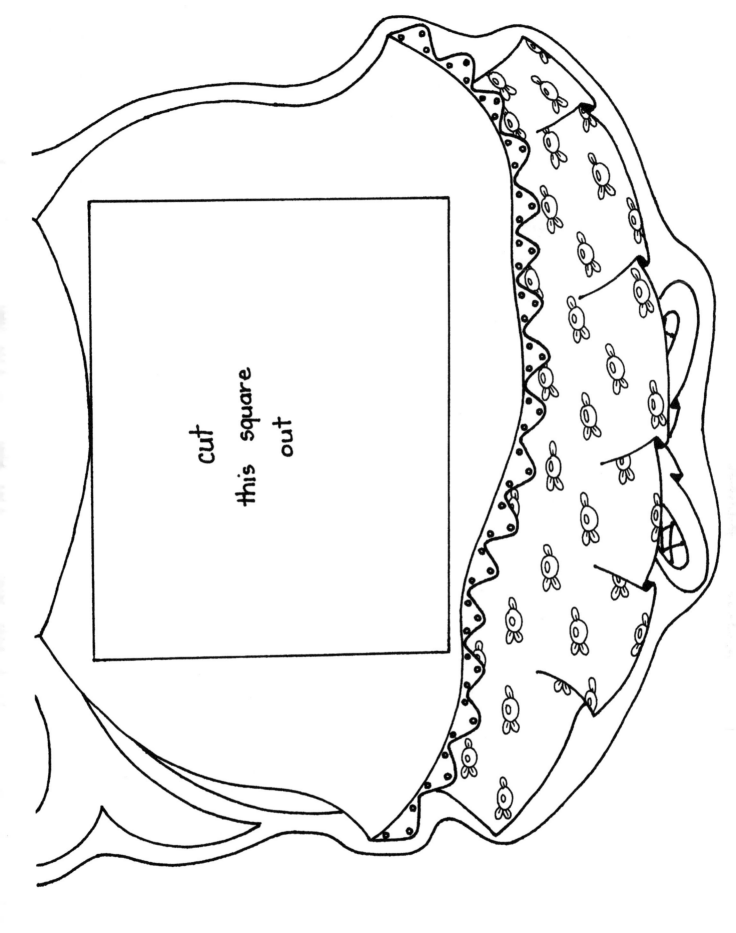

cut
this square
out

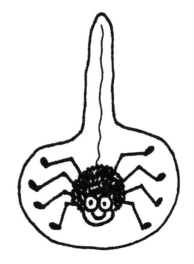

86

88